Masked Molestation

Copyright © 2012 by Dorothy Hall

All rights reserved. Published in the United States of America

Dorothy Hall Publishing

Augusta, GA

No part of this book may be reproduced, stored in a retrieval system, or transmitted by any means, electronic, mechanical, photocopying, recording, or otherwise, without written permission from the author.

Used by permission. Excerpt from *Holy Bible, Woman Thou Art Loosed Edition*
New King James Version
©1998 by Thomas Nelson, Inc.

Scripture taken from the New King James Version®. Copyright ©1982 by Thomas Nelson, Inc. Used by permission.

(Paperback)

ISBN-13: 978-1477534663 (CreateSpace-Assigned)

ISBN-10: 1477534660

Cover design by Lisa Sims
www.Passionate2design.com

First Edition October 2012

LCCN: 2012909756

Dedication

I'm sincerely dedicating this book to the prevailing adult victims of masked molestation and to the children who are enduring this heinous behavior. I hope and pray that your suffering will not be ongoing and that your masked molester will be apprehended and called accordingly to pay for his or her actions.

For all of the deplorable circumstances, ranging from being uprooted and placed in foster care or being placed with other unstable family members, to the heartbreaking mental anguish and the lifelong psychological impact that sexual molestation causes, know that our Father God is one who cannot lie. His word says that He will put no more on us than we can bear.

I send my love abundantly. God bless you, and may you be freed from bondage, for a weight such as this to be placed on one's shoulders is a weight that no one should have to bear for a lifetime.

TABLE OF CONTENTS

Chapter One
    My Daddy Shows Love Like This 1
    Comments..5

Chapter Two
    Didn't You Know You Were Hurting Me?....................8
    Comments..11

Chapter Three
    Mommy, Please I Need Your Help 14
    Comments..23

Chapter Four
    Hidden Tears of Lost Fruit 25
    Comments..27

Chapter Five
    A Daughter's Cry 30
    Comments..32

Chapter Six
    Results of Endurance through a Brother's Love 34
    Comments..40

Chapter Seven
    Grandpa and the Hottest Summer Ever 43
    Comments..56

Chapter Eight
    Uncle Jerry Taught Me to Drive...................................57
    Comments..62

Chapter Nine
    Misguided Divorce 63
    Comments..66

Chapter Ten
    A Letter to the People Who Hurt Me 67
    Comments..68

TABLE OF CONTENTS (continued)

Chapter Eleven
    Never Degrade Your Child 69

Chapter Twelve
    Searching for Daylight 72

Chapter Thirteen
    A Pretty Picture 73

Chapter Fourteen
    Almost Suffocated 74

Chapter Fifteen
    Don't Bond So Quickly With Strangers Around
    Your Children 82

Chapter Sixteen
    Paying Attention to Your Children 84

Chapter Seventeen
    Facts 86

Chapter Eighteen
    Scorned by the Devil's Advocates 88

Chapter Nineteen
    Seeking Help for a Breakthrough 89

Chapter Twenty
    Resolving the Issues 93

Chapter Twenty-one
    Organizations Offering Assistance 106

Conclusion 110

Inspiration

To my beautiful daughters, Rockell, Cleopatra, and Honeé Symone, I do all that I do for them. They are my world and what keeps me going.

Introduction

I have a child that dwells within me that is a victim of sexual molestation. When I was eight years old, I became a victim. At the age of twelve, I decided to take life into my own hands. I thought, What is my purpose for staying home? What could be worse than being a prisoner in my own home with no one to trust and no one to turn to? At least that was what I believed, but being in the streets wasn't as easy as I thought it would be. In fact, I got a lot more than I bargained for. Once I was in the streets, I realized there was no one I felt comfortable with nor trusted. In my eyes, everybody was my enemy.

Today as I write this book, I'm twenty-nine years old with two daughters, ages eight and eleven. I'm also incarcerated in a federal prison in Marianna, Florida, serving a ten-year sentence for a drug conspiracy charge.

Here at the prison camp, I participate in a program called G.O.A.L.S. (Gaining Options For Adapting Lifestyles). In this group, women discuss and process their issues and learn how to improve their lives. None of us could have imagined in a million years how deep we were going to have to dig in order to get to the core of our problems. In this program I have met some very interesting women who have shared their stories with me. Currently, I am a peer mentor for the future G.O.A.L.S. group and plan to continue my participation for the remainder of my sentence. It is necessary to mention the woman, Dr. Willis, the phenomenal psychologist who helps guide women through the program. She has been our light and guide to a better day.

One of the most valuable things I have learned from this program is humility. Being a victim of molestation had always been an embarrassment to me. I felt that I was alone. I had no idea I was not only surrounded by victims of molestation, but they had experienced even worse circumstances than I had. Together, we have learned how to cope and deal with our situation rather than keeping our secrets bottled up inside. Because an outlet for unresolved emotional pain is imminent, molestation victims can inadvertently self-inflict pain and/or sabotage their relationships. Therapy can be extremely beneficial.

It's been said that in the long run, hurt people will hurt other people, so an outlet is needed.

I felt it necessary to write this book, hoping to open the eyes of parents and loved ones who've been molested, and for those who might think this can never happen to them. From personally being in a situation such as this, I offer you this information.

Not everyone is capable of such heinous actions, but for those who are, we need to be aware. We need to have our eyes open to the safety of our innocent children who don't have a clue what this cruel world has to offer. We need to protect them to the best of our ability from the masked molesters in this world. They have no conscience. All they care about is fulfilling their disgusting sexual desires. My purpose isn't to scare parents, but to make those who have no clue become more aware.

Millions of people are already aware that sexual abuse is a worldwide subject today, but choose to ignore what's realistic. Statistics state that the average child molester will molest 50 girls before being caught and convicted. A child molester that seeks out boys will molest 150 boys before being caught and convicted, and he will commit at least 280 sexual crimes in his lifetime. Most sexual abuse happens between the ages of 7 and 13. There are over 491,720 registered sex offenders in the United States as of 2012. About 80,000 to 100,000 of the above offenders are missing. Molesters known by the family or victim are the most common abusers. The acquaintance molester accounts for 70-90 percent of reported cases. One out of six boys will be sexually assaulted before they reach the age of eighteen. Females are just as violent as male abusers. A study in 1993 found that adolescents were responsible for about one half of the child molestation cases and one-fifth of all rapes. This is one perpetrator we cannot forget when teaching our children what to watch for and what to do if someone tries to hurt them. Okay, if you don't want to think about it, at least take the time to really analyze the stories that lie between the pages in this book.

Absorb the stories as best you can. I want you to pay close attention to the mindset of abused children and its after effects as adults. Then I want you to think about what you can do to help minimize the attack of masked molesters.

I pray by the time you've completed reading this book, you'll think twice about the safety of innocent children.

I've had the opportunity to come into contact with many women that are still dealing with the tragedy of their childhood. Their stories are so completely different, but at the same time similar. You will witness this for yourself here in the stories. Either they tried to tell someone and no one believed them, or they were afraid to tell because the masked molester threatened to hurt someone dear to them. Some just kept quiet for unselfish reasons, being that their minds weren't advanced enough to know what was really going on even though they knew the encounter didn't seem right.

Many of these women are scorned to the point where they feel it is something they'll never be able to live with and let go. Others hate themselves because they feel embarrassed, as if they have done something wrong or could have done something to prevent this from happening. Some women say things such as a smell, a song, a reaction from a specific person, and even a touch that comes across the wrong way can trigger old, unwanted memories to awaken.

Some women are so afraid of even bringing up the subject of child molestation to the point where they say it makes their stomach churn and makes them want to vomit. They'd rather put it in the back of their minds and try not to remember.

From talking with these women, I can feel their hurt and pain crying out from the child buried within them, as if it were happening at that very moment they confided. As a result of being molested, some people tend to turn to other things to find comfort or in trying to forget the reality of the tragedy that's happened in their life. Even though scars heal physically, these kind cut so deeply, not even the best surgeon can repair them.

Over the years I've wondered why people were drawn to me with their problems, so willing to open up to a perfect stranger. But I've always seemed to find an answer to help them feel better by being assertive and also letting them know they are not the only ones coping with the things they have gone through. I've come across some serious hurdles growing up in the streets, and know firsthand, that is not the answer to being a victim of sexual molestation. I was a rebellious child who was quick to learn anything necessary to survive in the streets, as long as I was away from under my mother's wings. At the age of twenty I chose to leave home, doing whatever I had to do to survive. Some things were fully unexpected. I can't go back and rewrite the past, but I can strive for a better tomorrow. I've taken all the things I've gone through and used them to my advantage to help others. Today, I'm an over comer with the help of unconditional love and sisterhood.

This book is only the beginning of the help I intend to give others. Again, this book isn't meant to scare you from what can happen, but to get you to prevent it from happening repeatedly. The children of today and tomorrow are our light to a brighter future.

Take heed and be blessed!

Acknowledgments

To my parents Vermell Fargas and Artic Hall, thanks for giving me life. To my grandmothers, Mary Hall and Dorothy Glover, I love you. To Mr. Donnell Kelley, the sweetest man I know, thank you for giving me the beautiful Honeé Symone Kelley. To my editor, Mrs. Linda Wilson, author of *A Taste of Java*, I couldn't have asked for a better person to have on my team. To my cover designer, Lisa Sims, thanks for bringing my vision to life. Ms Sandi Collins, thanks for your insight. Mr. Jeffrey Hall, thanks for believing in my work and for your encouragement.

Serenity Prayer

God grant me the serenity to accept the
things I cannot change, courage to change
the things that I can, and the wisdom
to know the difference.

CHAPTER 1

MY DADDY SHOWS LOVE LIKE THIS

Mommy, Daddy loves me so much he does my hair and bathes me. Anytime something doesn't go my way, he rushes to my rescue. Sometimes when Daddy is late for work, he'll still volunteer to take me to school. Even if I'm sick and he knows he could lose his job, he'll stay at home with me anyway and let you go to work. When I want to cuddle with you, Daddy will say, "Mommy has worked too hard. Leave her alone so she can rest." Daddy tells me to go into my room and watch TV or something, and he'll come in to check on me and tuck me in when it's time for bed. Everybody in the neighborhood loves my daddy. They can see how much he loves me by all the time he spends with me.

When I'm alone sitting on the front porch, people (including my mommy), think I'm sad because of Daddy's absence. But I'm sitting on the porch filled with anger and rage because I'm heartbroken. I can barely sit on the porch because my bottom is so sore from Daddy playing with me. He says he's not trying to hurt me; he just loves me so much that he likes to play with me. Daddy tells me if anyone ever takes me away from him he'll die. I don't want my daddy to die. I love my daddy and Daddy loves me. When my bottom is sore I tell Daddy, and he checks on it when he's bathing me. Mommy never has to bathe me because Daddy always does it. He makes it all well, but then he makes it sore again. I know something is wrong, but I don't wanna question Daddy's love for me.

If I lose him, Daddy says I'll end up with people that won't feed me, people that will beat me and leave me in the backyard to sleep until daylight comes. I don't want those things to happen to me because I'm afraid of the dark and Daddy knows it. He leaves the light on for me before he tucks me in. When my daddy tucks me in, he doesn't just kiss me on the lips. Daddy kisses my entire body because he loves me. I know Daddy loves me, but why does it hurt worse this time? Daddy came into my room one night as I was crying and couldn't stop. I didn't want Mommy to hear me because she's so grouchy. She only fusses and calls me spoiled. She always tells Daddy to go check on his crying child. So my daddy comes in and says, "You know daddy loves you. What's wrong? You can't let your mom hear you crying. She'll only fuss at you. I don't want her to fuss at you." Daddy cuddles with me because he loves me. He even lotions my entire body, and he tells me other kids are ashy because their daddy's don't love them enough to spend time lotioning their body down. My daddy brushes my hair while I sit in front of the mirror as he kisses me on the neck, and then he tells me how much he adores me. My daddy shows me true love. Mommy never pays me any attention. Daddy lets me sit up in the middle of the night while Mommy is sleeping or working the midnight shift. Daddy lays his head in my lap and asks me to rub his head because he has a headache. He says I should be thankful because other kids don't even have a daddy. Daddy says he'll never leave me as long as I do what he asks me to do and never tell. It's our little secret and secrets never get told. Daddy says when Christmastime comes, he doesn't want to tell Santa that I've been a bad little girl, so be good so he can give me everything my little heart desires. I don't want to lose my daddy. I don't want my daddy to die. So I'm gonna be a good little girl.

At times when Daddy makes my bottom really sore, he fixes it. I want to tell somebody, but I am only seven years old. Who's gonna take care of me? Mommy doesn't have time, and nobody wants to be bothered with a seven-year-old child that cries herself to sleep every night. I wish somebody else loved me besides Daddy, and then my bottom wouldn't be so sore all the time. The pain is getting worse. I don't know how much more I can take. I couldn't even sit in the bath water because it hurt so bad. Somebody, please help me. I have a secret to tell about how much my daddy loves me.

Dorothy Hall

Chapter 1

(Poetic Pain)

My daddy shows love that doesn't come from up above.
Every time his kind of love rains down on me,
my bottom is filled with aches and pains.
Mommy neglects to check on me,
'cause Daddy expresses to her how much he loves me.
Daddy's destroying me, and he's not thinking twice of the innocence that he's stolen from me.
I cry for help from within, but nobody hears me.
Not even Mommy.
What must I do to take this pain away and escape this hidden misery?
Mommy, wake up.
PLEASE . . .
'Cause you cannot see.
Snatch off Daddy's mask
so that you can see what he's doing to me.
I need you.
PLEASE HELP ME!
Or am I to keep his hidden secrecy only to terrorize me?

Masked Molestation

Comments on Chapter 1:

Think about the title of chapter one and why the little girl expresses herself the way she does about her daddy. It is implicit how the mother must be thinking the dad adores the little girl so much. Not all dads behave this way. But in this situation, the dad's an awesome dad in the mother's eyes. The mother is neglecting a little girl that is crying out for help by allowing the daddy to take on all responsibility for the child. Daddy's facade is so flawless; Mom would never think he'd treat the child in such a cruel manner.

There's no irony here whatsoever.

The little girl is scared to death. She can't even distinguish between what's good and what's bad anymore. One minute she sees this perfect father figure, and the next minute the little girl is witnessing a man (unknown to her in a sense) removing a mask right in front of her eyes.

Daddy is not acting out of kindness or sincerity. He's not rushing to her rescue just because something's not going her way. He does this to protect himself because he's afraid she'll tell someone his dirty little secret. He wants to be in the girl's presence as much as possible, to always know what's going on with her, as well as letting the child know if there's a problem on her behalf, he will be the first one called to rectify the situation.

This is manipulating the child without threats. Automatically, the child is afraid to say anything, thinking her daddy would be furious with her if she ever told. Besides, no one would believe the child based on the concern he shows for her when they are in the presence of others.

Daddy doesn't mind giving her a bath when he's aware of the condition the child is in to keep the mother from finding out. Daddy is also quick to take the little girl with him when he's out with the fellows. Just another day of heinous acts carried out by the masked molester.

When the little girl is sitting on the porch, she is in deep thought of her enduring pain, not missing her daddy. But since Daddy has put on such a perfect facade, the people (including the mother), who are on the outside looking in, think it's because of the dad's absence. No one even bothers to find out what's wrong with the little girl. They only assume what they want to.

It's not good to always assume what's going on in someone's head. You could be far off base, even for a seven year old. Take the time out to ask the child what might be wrong instead of being arbitrary about the situation.

In chapter one, the dad is being so manipulative, he even states to the little girl that he's not trying to hurt her as he assures her how much he loves her. Someone has to intervene, letting the child know that love is not expressed like this.

The mom has given him total control. She has even come to the conclusion that the little girl's cry is a result of having been spoiled by the dad. Who could be so naive? The dad then goes to check in on the child, as if he doesn't know her reason for crying. He doesn't even give a sign, because he knows the crying is from the pain he's caused.

Masked Molestation

The child is so confused and trapped in a maze; she doesn't know where to begin to escape the pain from the walls built around her.

Chapter 2

Didn't You Know You Were Hurting Me?

You knew you were hurting me, but you couldn't care less. All you wanted was what you wanted. You never cared about the impact this hurt put on me. Nobody cared. No one looked my way. I was terrified, embarrassed. You hurt me so bad that I cried in the day and I cried in the night. I even cried when you were looking at me, but my tears were just on the inside. Oh my! If it were possible, I would've drowned in my own tears. For years I walked around mad at the world. Why?

Because you hurt me. Never will I be able to have children. You caused me to have a hysterectomy at an early age. I made bad choices because of my pain, and I hurt people because you hurt me. My heart is bitter and cold. In my eyes, all men are devils. That's not the way it's supposed to be just because one man hurt me. All men aren't the same as you, but you've set a bad example for the good men that are out there. I've tried sex with a man. Guess what? No pleasure for me. I don't even know what it feels like to be satisfied when I'm with a man. You knew you were hurting me. You deprived me of being a mother. I want to deprive you of the rest of your life, but I cannot do that because I'll go to prison. It's strange because you didn't go to prison. The people that loved you protected you. They wouldn't dare have let you go to prison. Did they listen to me? No. And you knew they wouldn't after you told them I had a boyfriend around the corner from where we lived. Never did I once have a boyfriend. *Never.* The nerve of you to take my womanhood from me and put it on an invisible boy around the corner. How dare you! You had everybody where you wanted them. You played all your puppets by their strings, and they all followed accordingly.

You had me trapped in a maze without knowing where to begin to get out. I felt like I was inside the little box presented on the movie *Hell Raiser*. I'm a grown woman now, but the little girl still lives inside me. The little girl thinks for me most of the time, because she's been through much more than I have as a woman. I can still hear her cries. But I'm being strong for her, because she never had anyone to be there for her in the beginning.

Everybody was against her. She had no one to turn to. It felt like she was always in a bottomless abyss with nothing to hold on to. Whatever happened to the invisible boy around the corner? He never showed his face.

Did I imagine all that had happened to me, not wanting to reveal the invisible boy? Was there someone holding me down aggressively in the back of a pick-up truck in the middle of nowhere gripping my hair tightly and telling me to stop screaming before he made the pain worse as he penetrated me? Was this just a figment of my imagination? Certainly, there was no boy around the corner. Was it my fault that my body developed quicker than the average eleven-year-old girl? No, but this masked man paid more attention to me than I paid to myself. I still adored my baby dolls at eleven. I enjoyed playing with Barbie and having tea with Raggedy Ann as she sat there listening to me talk about school and how happy I was to have a loving family. I was content with that. Then the masked molester came along and stole that all away.

He stole a bright future from me. I had such a rough time trying to get over all that had happened, scared that any man I came in contact with was subject to hurting me. It didn't matter what title he held, I still saw a masked man, and the only way to protect myself was to run and hide. He was a mean, mean man, standing in my face and calling me a liar once I confronted him. Oh my God, the shame I felt because nobody believed me. I asked, "Why won't anyone look for the boy around the corner?" They told me, "We're going get this all taken care of, and you better not go around the corner anymore with the little boy." I wasn't allowed any 'buts' when grown people were talking, so I dropped my head. They would take care of it like they said, without another word about it.

But that never happened. They swept it under the rug. I know I wasn't the first, and I wouldn't be the last victim of this masked molester. Eventually, I found out there were women in the family that had gone through the same thing. Did anyone speak up for me? No, that's why he still wears his mask today, because they allow him to.

Of course, the masked molester knew the pain he was causing. How could a grown man not know he's hurting a young girl? He didn't have a care in the world. All he cared about was fulfilling his sick sexual desires.

Comments on Chapter 2:

The grown woman in chapter two is expressing the pain she has carried with her for many years, and the scars still remain. It is just up to her how she is going to deal with this pain.

This woman hasn't been able to keep a stable relationship because of the impact of the hurt that remains from her past. Although she knows all men aren't to blame for what one masked man did years ago, she's having a hard time grasping the concept. One day the relationship may be going well, and the next day the man she's involved with may touch her the wrong way or wear a cologne that makes her past resurface all over again. It's a good thing she knows there are some good men out there in the world. But after having been scarred, it's hard not to look at the next man and wonder if he's capable of the same actions as the man who revealed his true self to her all those years ago.

She ponders why after having had sexual relationships she's unable to be fulfilled. At first she wonders if it is just her, or if the man she's involved with is incapable of getting her to climax.

Furthermore, what about the mental anguish she feels when she walks through the park and sees mothers out with their children? What about the many times she will stroll through the mall watching all the expectant mothers, and knowing the day will never come when a baby will exit her womb?

Even after experiencing all this torment and growing resentment, it is not a good idea for her to go around thinking of committing murder. What will that solve for her? "Premeditated" will probably result in her having to serve the rest of her life in prison. So once again, she allows the masked molester to have control over her. If she were to act on these thoughts, her life would be taken from her all over again.

In this chapter, the little girl that dwells inside the woman didn't have a boy that lived around the corner as a friend. A little boy never existed. Although young girls do interact with young boys, that doesn't mean they are having sexual relations. But it was so easy for the masked molester to create the little boy in his own image. That would make it easy for the people she thought she could trust to turn a blind eye and a deaf ear to what they didn't want to be true about the man they adored so much. Nobody even tried to locate the little boy. They were afraid to search because deep down inside they knew he never existed. That meant in their heart of hearts someone had to pay for the crime that had been committed.

Guard your child. Listen to them, pay attention to their physical and emotional state frequently.

Where's the little boy around the corner? He doesn't exist is the answer, so who is going to make the guilty pay?

Masked Molestation

Chapter 2

(Poetic Pain)

Amazing in a horrible way
How did they let this man take my dignity away?
The pain he caused drove me insane.
He stole my kangaroo pouch that will never poke out.
Other women make motherhood look so good,
but I'll never know the feeling,
not even after emotionally healing.
Instead I'm alone and left to cope with shameful memories,
and I'm losing all hope.
I can't even look at a man or have him touch me;
too haunted by the past and my hidden secrecy.
How can I help stop this from happening to others,
if they continue to let the masked man live undercover?
For heaven's sake,
don't make Heaven shake.
Bring him out; point him out,
so another little girl doesn't have to shout this out.

Chapter 3

Mommy, Please, I Need Your Help

My mother is getting old and my father is not attracted to her anymore. The body she had when they married doesn't exist now. They both drink heavily and they don't take care of themselves like they used to. My sister and I are their only two kids. Anything we do wrong, my father beats the hell out of us. Mom doesn't say anything because he beats the hell out of her too. Mom goes in the bathroom, cleans herself up, and resumes normal operations. Mom tells Destiny and me how much she loves our father and how she will do anything for him. Mom says he's only upset because he can't find a decent job to take care of home, and he feels like he's less than a man because she makes more money.

We live in a middle class community. Everyone sees our family as the perfect family. We have a three-bedroom, two-bath home with a basement and double car garage. A little dog named Spot, a Ford pick-up truck, and a fairly new Volvo, which is our family car. Mom is a registered nurse and has been for the past fourteen years. My father is always in between jobs.

My name is Faith and I'm thirteen. My sister is twelve. I have the same complexion as my father, and Destiny's tone matches our mother's. One dark-skinned, and one bright-skinned. My mom has always said that true love brought her and my father together. Mom used to spend so much time with us and act so different. Now it seems like she has changed within the blink of an eye.

Let me tell you the tragic story that goes on behind closed doors that nobody knows. It all started with our father mowing our lawn. Percy is his name. Destiny and I would take a shower one after the other. We both would get this strange feeling, like someone was looking in on us as we showered. The only person in our yard was Percy. "It couldn't be Daddy," I said. Destiny would agree, saying, "Of course not." Maybe it was a shadow and we both were mistaken. Still, we felt violated not knowing exactly what was going on. Every time we looked up, the shadow would disappear.

Our mom, Daisy, would come home and we'd tell her what happened. She said, "You and your sister are exaggerating. There's nobody looking in on you two. Nobody can get into the yard because the gate is always locked. Your father is in the yard all day, every day. He would've seen someone looking in on you two." Then she yelled, "By the grace of God, give me a break! Can't you see I just got off from work and I'm tired? On top of that, I have to cook. I don't wanna hear it anymore. You hear me?" Evidently, Mom discussed it with Percy. And Percy said, "That's nonsense. It must be a figment of their imagination."

The phone rang and it was another one of Percy's clients calling to cancel his services. Daddy was furious. I could tell by the anger covering his face. Mom looked a bit frightened as he slammed the phone down. Daddy looked at Mom and said with pure anger, "Isn't dinner ready yet? All this time you've been home." Mom smacked her teeth really hard as she rolled her eyes. Percy said, "Fuck it, I don't want the food. You eat it, with your fat ass. I don't know why I married you anyway. Look atcha'. Fat, sloppy, and sorry as hell. You can't even give me a good fuck anymore. If you don't get it together, one day soon I'm leaving your ass." Mom looked completely devastated.

She loved Percy so much she'd do anything to keep him, and even turned a blind eye and deaf ear to anything he'd do or say. Percy started drinking more than ever and coming home whenever he wanted. Mom didn't question him. Often, when she did try to be nice and find out where he'd been, Percy would get furious.

After a few weeks went by, the beatings started. Percy would haul off and slap Mom for no apparent reason. Daisy would grab her face and say, "Percy, why did you do that?" Percy would say, "Because you make me sick, bitch! I can do what I want in my house." Percy wasn't paying any bills, but he sure acted like he was. Mom was pulling overtime like crazy. Daisy didn't have a choice. Destiny and I had to start feeding ourselves using the microwave. We turned into great microwave cooks.

One day, Percy came in and asked Destiny and me what we were doing. Destiny would give him a nasty look, but I'd answer. I lost all respect for him, but had to show respect because he's my dad. Percy could never tell when I was angry with him. Unbelievably, I kept a smile on my face at all times. I didn't want Percy to know how afraid I was. I turned into a true master of disguise. Daisy would come in and drop her purse, kick off her shoes and hit the sack without a shower. She was so worn out she started to get blisters on her feet. We could see the look of exhaustion on her face.

Destiny and I didn't wanna bug her. But to feel her love, we'd go in her bedroom and cuddle underneath her as we watched her sleep. Percy sometimes came in and told us to get the hell out of there and go to our room. We'd exit Mom's room quietly, too afraid to say anything because we never knew what his reaction would be. Percy would wake Mom up telling her to give him sex. Destiny and I would be posted outside their bedroom door after he slammed it in our face. Destiny would sit there and cry. I'd try to keep her quiet and wipe the tears from her face. Little did we know that wasn't all that was going to happen in our perfect little home. The masked man was on the move. Once he started, our house quaked like it never quaked before. Mom was in her room crying continuously. We never saw her at that point. Percy came rushing out slamming the door behind him. All we could do was hear Mom crying. Percy looked at us, knelt down beside the door and said, "Get your asses away from the door now, and don't bother your mother!" As we headed for our room, Percy grabbed Destiny by the arm and said, "Bring your disrespectful ass with me." He took Destiny to the basement and closed the door behind him.

At first I just thought he took Destiny down there to talk. Never in my wildest dreams did I think Percy, our father, was having his way with Destiny in the basement. They stayed down there for three hours. Once Destiny came back up, there were no tears, no indication that he even touched her. She was just silent. I shook Destiny as she tried to walk past me looking like a zombie. I asked her, "What did Percy do?" Destiny never said anything, but one tear released itself from her right eye, rolling slowly down her cheek. That was one episode. It took Percy a while to bother me. I could never figure out why Mom never paid any attention to what Percy was doing. He completely distanced us from our mother.

One day when we came in from playing, we could hear Mom screaming, "Percy, don't do this. Please don't do this!" Their bedroom door was cracked. Destiny wouldn't go near the door. I was very inquisitive and wanted desperately to know why Daisy was begging Percy to stop. Silently, easing to the door, I stuck my head as close to the door as possible. I couldn't believe my eyes. Percy had Mom's arms tied to poles on the headboard and her feet to the poles at the foot of the bed. He held some type of object that appeared to be unpleasant to my mother. Quickly, I removed my face from the door with a fast paced heartbeat I couldn't get under control. Never knowing all this time that Percy knew I was peeping in their bedroom door and yet he still continued to do what he was doing to Mom.

Mom confused me, because I couldn't understand why she'd allow Percy to treat her this way. When I asked her about it, she said that she loved him and didn't want to lose him no matter what he had done. All I could think was, When was it going to be enough for Mom to wake up and smell the coffee? She doesn't need Percy. What's his purpose? No job, always drunk and abusing us all— mentally, physically and sexually. Percy started really getting out of control. Destiny and I were only kids. Mom wouldn't do anything to help us.

My sister and I were asleep late one night when Percy came into our room waking us. Mom was working overtime. Destiny and I both must have been in a deep sleep. Percy was pissy drunk as always. He came over to my bed unbuckling his belt buckle with a grin on his face, and allowing his pants to drop to the floor. Percy grabbed my bony little legs, flipping me over toward him and tearing my gown. Destiny turned her head and covered her ears. The only reason he tore my gown was to put fear in me. I was so terrified I didn't know what to do. I trembled as Percy covered my mouth and nose to keep me quiet. He almost suffocated me. I twisted and turned, trying to get him to stop, but it only hurt worse. I'd never felt a feeling such as that before. I can't even explain. I felt robbed of something I never knew I had. Percy continued penetrating me as all of his sweat dripped from his forehead and his smelly alcoholic breath covered my face. I'd cried before from being hurt with a busted knee, a broken arm, and even a first degree burn, but never had I ever felt pain to this magnitude. When Percy released himself from me, all I could do was turn over onto my side, grab the pillow from my bed, and bite into it as I screamed.

Once Percy wasn't in sight anymore, Destiny came to comfort me to the best of her ability. She knew the pain I was enduring. Destiny never spoke of her pain. But now, I knew firsthand what she was dealing with. Destiny and I had a long talk. We decided to tell Mom what was going on. Daisy started making excuses as we explained to her down to the very last detail to convince her we were telling the truth. Daisy said she was sorry she hadn't been spending a lot of time with us and that she was going to take us shopping. She told us she was going to take a week off just for us. I was like, "Momma, please stop it."

Mom said, "No, you stop it. Never ever say things like that about your daddy ever again."

At that very moment, I wanted to slap my own mother for not seeing my father for what he really was. Destiny and I both felt the pain our father bestowed upon us. But for our mother not to believe us felt like we'd been shot in the heart with a bow and arrow.

Daisy told us to keep our mouth closed before we make her look bad and the Department of Family and Children Services come out to investigate our home. Daisy said she'd lose everything behind this foolishness we were talking. She said for us just to listen to our father and do whatever he says, and don't question him. It was like she gave him permission to do whatever he wanted.

Percy took his turn from Destiny to me. Destiny never spoke a word again. I had to find some sort of outlet. I couldn't bury myself underneath this madness. I started sneaking out to find some sense of peace other than being at that house. Percy would come looking for me to beat me all the way back home. Destiny would never leave because she was scared. It's a pity how our home became a dungeon to her, but also her comfort zone.

Percy made her so crazy; she couldn't distinguish between the two. The last time Mom heard about Daddy penetrating us wasn't from us. She saw it with her own

Masked Molestation

eyes. Percy came home one day calling out to us. We wouldn't answer. Percy called again, "Faith, Destiny, you have ten seconds to get out here or I'm beating some ass today." We came and Percy said, "So you told your mom on me, huh? What did I tell you would happen if you told your mom?" Percy was drunk and had a gun. At first, we thought Percy was gonna kill us. Percy waved Destiny over to him with the gun, telling her to perform oral sex on him. When he was tired of her, he called me over to do the same thing. We both were on our knees with Percy standing there with no clothes on with his penis in my mouth. Mom came home early from work, busting through the door and catching Percy dead wrong.

Destiny and I were both so happy. We thought it was over until Daisy turned a blind eye and walked back out the same door. She left as if nothing had happened.

Chapter 3

(Poetic Pain)

My father's child.
My God! It's about to drive me wild.
My child,
born into the world by the same seed that produced me.
I know Heaven's looking down to see.
I had a choice to water the seed or kill it.
I thought of killing the seed,
because I thought it would set me free.
But soon I realized this seed, too, was a part of me.
"Help me, Father, please!"
I prayed as I knelt in shame and the embarrassment that covered me.
Then I decided to nurture the seed,
not wanting it to become like the monster that planted the seed in me.
My mother,
the woman that carried and nurtured her own seed,
turned a blind eye and a death ear to something she didn't want to believe.
My mother left her two seeds lonely and afraid,
confused and abused, with a ticking time bomb that needed to be defused.
What were we to do?

Comments on Chapter 3:

I bet you are wondering what happened to Faith and Destiny. Well, let me fill you in. Faith became pregnant and her mom made her get an abortion.

Destiny was five months pregnant during the time Faith was taken for an abortion. No abortion for Destiny. At the age of thirteen, she gave birth to her father's daughter.

Everyone in the home pretended as if nothing had happened and the mother allowed the father to remain in the home.

No one ever acknowledged the child as the father's child. Destiny had to put her childhood aside to raise a child that was hers, as well as the child being her sister.

How do you think a thirteen-year-old child copes with something to this extent?

The mother and the father should have been made to pay for the pain caused on these two girls. But, no. Because nobody knew since it was a hush-hush thing in the family.

I know it's been said in many families, *What goes on in the home stays in the home.* But let's be for real here. This isn't something anyone should keep quiet about. It's only something to save face for the person committing heinous actions at the expense of an innocent child. Is saving face more important than a little girl's dignity? Where are the morals being taught here?

These parents aren't showing them what life is about. First impressions mean a lot in this world today, and what these girls experienced firsthand is a life full of pain, deceit, and betrayal!

This is not what life is supposed to be about. Yes, everybody has their ups and downs in life, but to this degree? No! It's just not meant to happen this way.

We must do everything in our power to protect the innocent from the masked molesters.

Chapter 4

Hidden Tears of Lost Fruit

I was fresh and ripe and now I've been bruised. I have nicks and scratches all over me. They gave me away. Truly, I'm scorned. Why didn't they know how delicate I was before they shipped me away? Strangers only cut the pieces out of me that they wanted. Then they chewed them up and spit it out.

Just when my parents thought they were doing the right thing when they gave me up for adoption, I'd been from pillar to post.

The first home I lived in, I can't remember what happened. It wasn't until I was five years old when I began to learn the cruelness of this world I live in. It makes me wish I could crawl back into my mother's womb where it's safe from the demons that come out of darkness. It's not true that freaks just come out at night. They live in the day also. They just wear masks to hide who they really are. I'm a victim of what's behind the mask. I have seen them in daylight, but nobody believed me. When I tried to point them out, people only thought I was crazy. All I could think of as I looked to the people that stood above me was, Wake up, you're the crazy ones. Not me. Can't you see what I see behind the mask? This person hurt me. I have the evidence in my underwear buried between my box springs and mattress in my room. I was afraid to show them to anyone because of the stains. I didn't want anyone to think I was a dirty little girl. But only to see that I'd been bruised between my thighs and it hurts.

At the age of nine my foster parents would try to manipulate me with ice cream, cake, and the movies. My foster father and I watched *Shrek* alone. He was so nice to take me. Just as the movie was getting good and I thought I was safe, he reached over, grabbed my hand and applied Vaseline to it. I was scared, shaking in my pants and thinking, same episode, different masked man. He didn't bruise me between my legs. He unzipped his pants, releasing himself as he placed my five little fingers around his penis. I didn't have a tight enough grip, so he squeezed my wrist to signal me, so no attention was drawn to us. At the age of nine, I was taught to massage a grown man's penis until he was satisfied. I never looked over at him. I continued to watch *Shrek* even though it wasn't making me smile anymore. Even the funny parts had tears rolling down my face. The most disgusting part was when he reached over as I was massaging him, rubbed the falling tears from my cheek and kissed me in the mouth.

My foster mother would always ask why I cried so much when Daddy was so good to me. I told her he hurt me. She said, "Nonsense. Is this how you repay us for all we've done for you?" Something deep down in my heart told me she already knew what the masked man was capable of doing. My foster mother helped him renew his mask every time they adopted another child.

Somebody, please take the mask off the molester so he can pay for his crimes.

Comments on Chapter 4:

Here's a confused child in chapter four whose biological parents thought giving her up for adoption would be the right thing to do.

In a way, the girl blames her parents. She thinks that if only they had given her a chance. She knew for certain it couldn't have been worse than what she was facing in a foster home the biological parents thought she'd be better off in.

Do you know how it must feel to wish you could crawl back into your mother's womb so it would protect you from the world at the age of five?

Each family she was placed with had a masked molester. And one family, since she was already so scorned by the others, was unable to figure out what was going on and she was too afraid to speak about it. They felt she was unhappy to be there. Then they placed her back into foster care in return for a child who seemed happy to live in their home.

The other families ignored the possibility of foul play, not wanting to expose their own family to any cruel actions. And the only ones that were aware without a doubt in their mind protected their own and returned her to the adoption agency.

For a five year old child to see the world as cruel with no other potential good things to offer has to be a scary thing no adult could imagine running through the mind of a child this age. The only worries a child of five should have is bedtime and going to school the next day.

The child tried to reveal the masked molester for who he really was. She explained in chapter four how the people thought she was crazy or just called her crazy to make her think whatever happened to her on their watch was an illusion.

This is what the child meant when she stated she'd seen them in daylight, when the masked molester only wants to reveal himself in darkness. But just as the saying, "What happens in the dark comes to light" is true. It is also true that when the molester is brought to light in the victim's eyes, it is often a task getting someone to believe them.

This chapter makes you question how much work these parents put forward to appear as "the perfect parents" to place a child with, only to later abuse them.

What kind of individual would pre-plan to take Vaseline to a movie with a five-year-old child?

Shrek is a movie that makes you laugh and cry, depending on how sensitive you are. This little girl had mixed emotions as she pretended in the sight of others to be enjoying the movie.

Chapter 4

(Poetic Pain)

Given away like an unwanted cloudy day.
Maybe I wasn't what they called sunshine and blue-skies
that brightened up their day.
Adopted into a thorn bush of dead roses
Every day I had to pay for that one cloudy day.
Stung by thorns and faced with the masked man's horns
looking down on me.
How do I escape back into the womb that carried me?
There, I know I'll be free from any pain or misery
As long as the mother of the womb is drug free
Woe is me.
I look up above and say, "Father, for heaven's sake,
you're the only one that can help me.
From this great evil, please deliver me.
Everyone else acts as though they can't hear nor see."

Chapter 5

A Daughter's Cry

The girl that lives within me is still crying. For many years I've buried the sound of her cries, and so did my mother. The thought of my mother hearing her cry as I do today and did nothing about it is absurd. Why wouldn't she listen to her daughter's cry? Did she love her boyfriend that much that she'd ignore a daughter's cry? My God, what has this world come to? Does it take a little girl to satisfy a grown man's needs when he has a full-grown woman lying beside him every night to fulfill his needs? Were my cries ignored because my mother knew this was a sick man, and this is what kept him home?

It wasn't only a sick man, but a sick woman. What kind of woman holds her little girl as she wipes the tears from her eyes, never asking where the tears are coming from? Maybe she's too afraid to ask the little girl. I know she couldn't have been more afraid than the little girl inside me was each and every time she endured the violating of her innocent body. I know she wasn't more afraid than that. The little girl has cried an ocean, not a river. She's drowning in her own tears. Nobody listened. Nobody threw in a life jacket to help save her.

Imagine being out in the middle of the ocean in the midst of the night on a ship. At first, everything is going right for you. You look around and there are people there whom you feel safe and protected by, but the grim reaper, AKA masked man, is still stirring close by, but you never saw him coming. You're laughing, playing, talking, and there's a sparkle in your eyes. The ship's lights are lit up everywhere. You're in the pool with several people playing with different sized beach balls. One of them rolls away and you're the one that volunteers to retrieve it. The ball is constantly rolling as you follow behind it trying to catch up. As soon as you kneel to pick it up there's the masked man. He's revealing his face to you, although you don't get a chance to tell anyone else. But even if you did, they can't seem to look behind the mask to see what you saw. Suddenly, he throws you overboard and nobody is there to throw you a life jacket. The ship has left. Nobody knows you're out there. Left to drown, hoping someone will come rescue you, you're in this endless body of water all by yourself.

Imagine the process of drowning. The feeling of suffocating inside your own body and your lungs wanting you to gasp for the air you'll never be able to take in. Your body is losing all consciousness. You can't even hear your own cries anymore. The worst part of it all is the fact that death never does overtake you.

These feelings you have to endure for the rest of your life or until you find some sort of outlet so that a major breakthrough frees the little girl crying within you. If only my mother had heard her daughter's cry. Everything beyond that cry could have been eliminated.

Dorothy Hall

Comments on Chapter 5:

Chapter five blatantly tells about a little girl searching for infinite peace with no understanding of the trials she's had to encounter throughout her life.

In becoming an adult, it's clearer to her what she's suffered as a child. Now she searches for reasons why a mother would knowingly allow her lover to repeatedly take advantage of her daughter. Deep down inside, the little girl knows the mother is aware of what she's going through, but she also knows she doesn't care as long as it keeps her mate home.

You can feel the little girl's pain by reading chapter five. Who wants to suffocate in their own tears? Even though the drowning didn't literally happen, the suffering was so severe this is the only way she could express her pain and emotions about something of this magnitude.

Chapter five also speaks about the grim reaper. In everyday life, the grim reaper is spoken of when pertaining to death. That's exactly what the little girl was feeling, as if she was suddenly taken by an unknown form to a deserted place where she would die. Who wants to live in agony, feeling that someone is sucking the life out of you daily and feeling your lungs collapsing, unable to grasp that last breath that keeps you alive.

Chapter 5

(Poetic Pain)

The story of the untold needs to unfold
Tears seep from within
My masked molester is my kin.
How can I stand
when I don't understand the problem at hand?
Just an innocent little girl.
Despicable things such as this destroys her world
Today, I still hear the little girl's cry
No one was there to save her from her own cries.
I even feel the pain of when she felt like she wanted to die.
No one to ease the pain
No one to shelter her from the rain
No one went to her rescue to say,
"It's okay and I'm here. I'll take away your rainy days."
No one to hold her and say,
"Place your precious head on my shoulder,
and the days will get better as you grow older."

Chapter 6

Results of Endurance through a Brother's Love

My name is Kenny. At the moment, I'm at the end of a dark road and staring death in the face. I've made some bad decisions that will eventually cost me my life. People always judge me, but they've never walked in my shoes. So who are they to judge me?

Everybody has gone through some kind of hardship in their life, and those who haven't are sure to go through some drama. All problems and struggles are not the same, but if you choose the wrong path, the decision you make could be detrimental.

I want to share a story with you about my masked molester.

When I was ten, I created a new identity for myself by changing my name to Kimmy. Kenny is my birth name, but I let my imagination get the best of me, so I could better cope with what I was going through. I wanted to believe I was a woman put on this earth to please men's sexual desires.

My masked molester was cruel, heartless and an alcoholic. He used his drinking as a facade.

Casanova is his name. Some consider him to be a real ladies' man. He always ran to everyone's rescue when they were in need. Those people never knew the man behind the mask. It's more dangerous when you don't know what you're dealing with versus dealing with someone you know is capable of murder. Your guard will be up for that person at all times, but when a nice, clean cut gentleman with all his ducks in a row enters your life, all guards are down.

Don't you know anybody and everybody is capable of doing something unethical? Maybe not to the same magnitude as Casanova did to me, but still, everyone has been disappointed and hurt by someone else's actions, even if its simplified to the least common denominator like: someone not washing their hands after using the restroom although they know they are going to serve food.

Casanova was a good husband and father for many years. All of a sudden, he started drinking. My mother made every excuse in the world for him, starting with her making more money than he did. Mom said Casanova felt less than a man because he brought home less money. Okay, Mom made excuses, but isn't marriage about togetherness? Mom wasn't concerned. Why couldn't Casanova just find a better job? It didn't take a rocket scientist to know any job that works around weather is bound to have its good days and bad days. You've got to be willing to take the bitter with the sweet. My brother Derrick and I couldn't understand the way things in our home took a turn for the worst.

Casanova began mentally abusing Mom, and then it became physical. At this point, Casanova didn't touch my brother and me. All we had to do was stay out of his way.

Casanova would beat Mom so badly she couldn't go to work some days because of the black eyes and busted lips. Yet, Casanova would still insist on getting sex from Mom after the beatings. If she refused, he'd take it. My brother and I felt so sorry for Mom even though she pretended as if everything was fine. My brother, Derrick was growing bitter inside. He'd draw pictures of Casanova hanging from a tree or plastered up against the wall with men surrounding him with bows and arrows. I'd hide the pictures to keep Casanova from finding them.

One stormy night, a black cloud covered our home and the storm stayed longer than expected. Derrick began acting out. When Casanova would beat Mom, Derrick would throw things and turn the music up loud to withdraw Casanova's attention from our mother. Usually, Casanova would ignore Derrick, but this particular night Casanova went into Derrick's room to punish him. It wasn't the usual father-son punishment.

Casanova brutally punished Derrick, beating him first. Then he forced him to remove his clothing. Derrick thought Casanova was only going to beat him naked, but he was in for a rude awakening.

Casanova told Derrick to turn around and put his hands on the bed. Casanova had him positioned on the bed as if he was an officer getting ready to frisk him. Derrick obeyed. Although he was already bruised from the previous beating, he removed his clothes. Casanova stood behind Derrick in cowboy position, unleashing his belt and releasing himself to penetrate Derrick. If only someone could have heard his screams.

I was the oldest, so I felt the need to protect my brother and my mother. I knew firsthand the pain Derrick was feeling. I'd already felt it; I just never said anything. What could my mother do to protect me? She was afraid of Casanova.

To keep Casanova from abusing my brother, I went to him and told him anytime he wanted me I wouldn't put up a fight, just leave Derrick alone. Casanova never answered me; he just looked and then walked away.

For a while, Casanova would call me into his room and I'd go willingly. Something must've changed or Casanova grew tired of me. He went into a rage, beating Mom and us, and forcing us into sexual encounters with him regularly.

Derrick was in such pain, I knew I had to do something. He could barely sit down. When taking baths, he'd sit down sideways in the tub. The bitterness grew deeper with much anger pasted on Derrick's face daily.

Casanova started favoring me because I'd cooperate when he wanted me. I didn't want to be beaten, and I felt at the time there was nothing I could do to stop him. I even volunteered to take my brother's place to keep him from hurting him. Even though I was enduring the same pain myself, I didn't feel the need for both of us and our mother to suffer. Over time, I became accustomed to what Casanova was doing. I couldn't beat him, so I had to join him. Nobody paid attention to what went on in our home. The masked man was allowed to keep his mask on until our last encounter with him.

Mom had been telling us everything was going to be all right, just bear with her. She told us our father wasn't as bad as he seemed. Repeatedly, she told us not to tell anyone about anything that went on in our home, so we didn't. But did she really know what was going on in our home?

Casanova came home totally out of control one day. Derrick was ignoring him. Casanova called out to Derrick. Instead of coming, he went into his room and slammed the door. Casanova became furious and frustrated with Derrick's reaction. There was nothing I could do or say to keep Casanova from attacking Derrick this particular night.

Casanova grabbed the doorknob to open Derrick's bedroom door. Finding it locked, he then reared back and kicked the door open. I followed Casanova, begging him not to hurt Derrick. Casanova hit me so hard, I flew backward as my head hit the edge of the coffee table, landing me in the corner. That's where I remained balled up in a knot crying as I watched Casanova beat Derrick and roughly penetrate him.

The most tragic thing happened that night. Mom came home and caught Casanova penetrating Derrick, who was screaming with his teeth locked tightly together. All I could say was, "Papi, please stop." I could see blood draining from Derrick's backside.

Mom stood there for a second in shock, and then headed for Casanova with anger, screaming, "You bastard! You dirty bastard!"

Casanova quickly turned to defend himself against Mom, his penis slinging away from my brother's anus. I shot toward Derrick to comfort him, but all I received was crying and rejection. I could feel hatred seeping from Derrick as he looked at me with careless eyes. Casanova continued beating Mom. The last blow to her head paralyzed her and left her in a coma that eventually resulted

Masked Molestation

in her death. Casanova received a life sentence in prison for murder and child molestation.

Derrick was taken to the hospital and needed sixty-four stitches in his rectum. Casanova was allowed to wear his mask for many years, while taking away our dignity. Now I'm a homosexual, trying to get my life together as I stare death in the face while suffering with the HIV virus. I made the wrong choice, but it was all I knew from my upbringing, and I lived my life recklessly, not worrying about tomorrow.

Parents, pay attention to your children, please. Once you have children, it's not about you anymore. Please don't let this happen to your child.

Yes, Casanova knew right from wrong, and that's why he used alcohol to cover up his true, sick addiction.

Comments on Chapter 6:

It has to be out of pure love that a child of Kenny's age would act on behalf of his mother and younger brother by giving himself to the father in return for keeping them from the father's wrath and untoward behavior.

This wasn't Kenny's job. It was the mother's responsibility to remove them from the home. Instead, she stayed and endured the abuse brought against her.

By the boys witnessing this behavior from Casanova and the mother, a seed was already planted to make them believe Casanova was superior and the mother inferior, leaving them with no one to turn to.

It's strange though how things turned out. Derrick wanted to protect the mother, and Kenny wanted to protect both the mother and Derrick. But Derrick didn't see it that way and turned against his brother. It wasn't even about Kenny. It was about the anger Derrick allowed to build up inside from everything he'd suffered. Sometimes it's hard to differentiate all the mixed emotions going on inside your mind and body without help.

Occurrences of this nature can put people on a good or bad path in life considering how they cope with it. Kenny proceeded without caution and ended up with the HIV virus because he turned cold and thought he only knew how to please men.

Derrick, on the other hand, grew bitter inside and despised homosexual men. He departed from his family and disowned his brother.

These boys lost two parents in a matter of minutes, causing them more pain on top of what they had lost over the past twelve months.

Dorothy Hall

Chapter 6

(Poetic Pain)

Bitter
Treated like an old piece of litter
Made a decision and changed my identity
This, I thought was what life meant for me to be,
A strong woman who others wouldn't forsake,
A regretful and terribly horrific mistake
I became my worst enemy giving myself an identity,
chosen by reason of my own misery
My pain and my shame
Caused by a father who was insane in the brain
The biggest cost
A life lost
The struggle of a mother taking matters into her own hands,
after catching the masked molester doing something she couldn't stand.
Mute and distant, the end result of abuse.
One brother accuses the other of not saving him from their father's misuse.
To sacrifice a body, some things will never be understood,
especially by one who's filled with so much hurt and shame
It takes them longer to overcome their pain.

Chapter 7

Grandpa and the Hottest Summer Ever

Too ashamed and embarrassed to tell my story, and as a result, many more little girls have been abused. I didn't want anybody to know it had happened in my home, because my child being molested on my watch was the last thing I thought could ever happen. Till this very day my heart is still troubled, even though the man was arrested and called accordingly to pay for his actions. I sit around wondering how I could have been so stupid not to pay more attention to my daughter. I could have gone public and become an advocate for children who were being molested under their parents' nose, but still I did nothing. My job wasn't more important than securing the safety of my daughter. We were a family of three, my husband Jeff, my daughter Jessica and myself. Neither Jeff nor my parents were alive. Jeff drove long haul for C&C trucking company and we barely saw him.

Hoping to take some of the financial strain off Jeff, I decided not to be a stay at home mom anymore and found a job. We had two new vehicles and a new home to pay for. Finally, I found a job doing shorthand and typing.

The job paid well. I was even able to pay a sitter to come into my home to look after Jessy. Everything started to take a turn for the better. Six months passed and things were still running smoothly. We began getting acquainted with our neighbors and the people in our community.

Everyone checked out to be a perfect law-abiding citizen, so to speak.

But then the bomb went off without warning. Jessy and I encountered the masked man, a sixty-two year old, well-groomed church going man. Everyone in our community adored the ground he walked on. All the children loved him dearly. They were excited every time they saw him. They'd have an enormous Kool-Aid smile plastered on their little faces, and greeted him with a hug. "Grandpa, Grandpa," they'd say as he swept them off their feet one by one, giving them a great big hug, a kiss on the cheek and a lollipop from his pocket.

The children's reaction made the parents feel safe and secure with him. The parents even called him Grandpa.

Never in a million years would I have thought that I would be the one removing the mask from a sixty-two-year-old grandpa to discover the misery that lay beneath.

The other parents' reactions allowed me to let my guard down and feel safe with Grandpa. I mean, who in the world would have ever seen it coming? I've learned never to judge a book by its cover. Read it or leave it alone. You need to know its contents before drawing a conclusion on whether it's good enough or not. For another year or so, every family in our community seemed happy and content. The kids were always happy and more excited when they had a chance to visit with Grandpa. They'd even come home with countless goodies and gifts. Grandpa had a playground in the backyard and a pool three-feet deep, assuring us safety for the children. Jessy would come home and talk me to death about Grandpa. I'd sit there and give

Masked Molestation

her my undivided attention, but my mind sometimes wandered to the idea of how great of a caregiver she would have if her biological grandpa were living, but since he wasn't I was blinded to think the masked man stood in just fine. And like many parents in my neighborhood who allowed Grandpa to babysit their children, I followed suit.

One afternoon I was running extremely late. My sitter didn't show up, nor did she think to pick up the phone to call me. All of my neighbors were working or either away from their homes. My first thought was Grandpa, but before I took Jessy over to his home, I consulted with her first. Jessy was very pleased at the idea. I went over and asked Grandpa would he be willing to watch Jessy. As I told him my situation, he never hesitated. He smiled and greeted Jessy as usual. Grandpa also offered to watch Jessy anytime I needed, telling me it wouldn't be a problem. I told him that was very nice of him and maybe I'd consider. I kissed Jessy on the cheek as I rushed off for work. I was so naïve and never thought twice about it. However, I called every hour to check on Jessy. She was fine and there was no indication at this point that I needed to be worried about anything out of the ordinary.

A few months down the line, I went into Jessy's room and found her playing with Barbie and Ken in an awkward manner. I stood there for a minute or two, and then I approached her softly. "Jessy, what are you doing to the dolls and why are you playing with them like that?" Jessy had the dolls fondling one another at first, and then sat Barbie on Ken's face. As I stood there those few minutes,

Jessy continued to fondle and caress the dolls as she had a conversation with me.

Jessy responded, "Oh, Mommy I'm just doing what Grandpa does to me when I spend time with him." At that moment I didn't know what to think because Jessy showed no physical signs of anger or abuse, nor did she speak in a harsh way about Grandpa.

My heart squealed in my chest. My stomach became nauseous and my eyes began to water. Quickly, I removed myself from Jessy's room, rushing to the restroom to release the boiling nervousness that conjured up into my stomach. Standing in the bathroom with my back up against the wall and knees shaking uncontrollably, I was trying my hardest to regain my composure before approaching Jessy again. Coming to my senses and trying to rationalize the situation, I went to call my husband. Not wanting to shake him up and put him in a state of shock, I decided not to call. I found myself slouched down next to the coffee table, trying to figure out whom to call.

I could hear a car pulling up and thought it was the masked man next door. Instead, it was Helen, my neighbor from across the street. I needed someone to confide in, someone that would feel the same way about this man as I did.

I called out to Helen as I stood in my doorway. "Helen, Helen, do you have a minute so that I may speak with you?"

"Yes, Sarah, what is it?"

"It's about my daughter, Jessy, and Grandpa."

Helen grabbed me by both of my arms.

"Sarah. First, slow down. You're shaking like crazy. What is it? Do you wanna come inside so we can talk?"

"Yes, I mean no. I can't leave Jessy. She's in the house alone. Do you mind coming over here?"

"No, I don't mind at all. What's got you so bothered?"

"Just come in and have a seat. I'll explain, and maybe you can tell me what I should do."

"Do about what, Sarah? Tell me what's going on here."

"Today I went into Jessy's room and found her playing with her dolls in an inappropriate manner."

"Is that what has you so worked up? I've found Amber doing that several times."

"Did you ever ask her why she does that?"

"No, why should I ask her? It's a normal thing for kids to do."

"Yes Helen, in some cases, but not this one. I asked Jessy why she was doing that to the dolls. Jessy said, 'It's what Grandpa does to me.'"

"She meant Ken is Grandpa and Barbie is her."

Helen dropped her keys. It looked like I had to pick up her bottom jaw. There was complete silence, not a word out of Helen. I could see it in her eyes and facial expression that she was hoping what I was saying didn't have any truth to it. One tear eased from Helen's right eye and glided down her cheek. At that moment, I knew she believed me and I'd confided in the right person. Helen started to mumble words from her lips.

"Sarah, if this is true, we need to follow proper procedure before confronting that dirty old bastard."

"What do you suggest we do first?"

"First, you get Jessy ready. I'm gonna go pick Amber up from my sister's house. Better yet, you two come and go with me to pick Amber up, and then we're going to the hospital. Then after we get some test results, we'll call the authorities."

Helen and I gathered up both children. They didn't have a clue what was going on. We didn't bother to ask them questions because we didn't want to confuse them.

Once we reached the hospital, we asked to consult with the attending physician on duty. Instead of going through so much red tape, we went straight to the hospital superintendent after talking with the doctor.

The doctor instructed the RN to immediately get separate rooms available for the girls. Then the doctor came over to us to explain what had to be done next.

"Ladies, I know you both are in a state of shock right now, but there's more that has to be done when I'm overseeing cases of this nature. It's my sworn duty to contact child services as well as the authorities." We agreed with the doctor, but we both were extremely concerned, worrying about what the social worker and authorities would think. We definitely didn't want them to think we abused our own children, nor did we want them to take the girls away from us. Helen and I talked back and forth with one another, because we'd never been in a situation like this before. We did agree on one thing, and that was the safety of our girls.

The lady from children services and the authorities arrived at the same time. The girls had been out of our care for about twenty minutes. I can't remember who started talking first, Helen or me. The officer said, "Okay, okay ladies, one at a time. Better yet, one of you can go with Mrs. Foster. The other can come with me. We're both going to need individual statements from you both. After that, we'll consult with the doctor and reach a conclusion from there. Are we all on the same page here?" Everyone responded yes at the same time. I went with Officer Bradley while Helen went with Mrs. Foster.

Officer Bradley asked me a series of questions and flipped them around as if they were different questions. I felt like he was patronizing me with this line of questioning, or he thought I'd done something to my own daughter. He was being so transparent.

I could see Helen standing about eight feet away from me, throwing her hands up and rubbing them through her hair. Her body language clearly explained she was lost and afraid of the current circumstances. When the questioning and statements were completed, they allowed us to go in to visit with Amber and Jessy. Their rooms were two doors from one another on opposite sides of the hallway.

I entered the room Jessy was being held in. A two-way mirror hung midway on the wall. Jessy was sitting there dressed in a hospital gown covered with cartoon characters and playing with toys and drinking a four-ounce cup of orange juice. She seemed so calm and happy. As soon as Jessy saw me, she gave me a big smile and walked over to hug me. She was holding a doll in each of her hands, one female doll and one male doll.

"Hello Jessy. Were you okay while mommy talked to the officer?"

"Yes, Mommy, they were really nice to me."

"Who was nice to you?"

"The nurses and the man with the white coat with the thing hanging around his neck."

"The man with the white coat is a doctor, Jessy."

"Oh yeah, he did say he was a doctor. The doctor listened to my heartbeat and he said I have a strong heartbeat."

"That's good. It means you're a healthy young lady."

"Mommy, that's not all he did. He checked me everywhere. The doctor even touched me where Grandpa touched me, but it was different and the nurse held my hand."

Listening to my daughter still refer to that dirty bastard as 'Grandpa' made me want to kill him. I didn't want to upset Jessy. All I could do was pull her into my arms and give her a warm embrace.

Apparently, the doctor had already done a thorough examination. "That was sweet of the nurse to hold your hand while the doctor checked you."

"Ooh and Mommy, she gave me orange juice, too."

"That was really nice of her. Did you thank her?"

"Of course I did, Mommy. Grandpa gives me nice things when he keeps me, and he always reminds me to say thank you. Grandpa said that if I'm a good little girl and I don't make any mistakes when we're playing 'Simon Says' that he'll give me nice treats and tell you how good I was when you come to pick me up." I swallowed the lump in my throat as my heart pounded. I tried to stay as calm as possible, not wanting to upset Jessy before she showed me exactly how she was taught to play Simon says.

"Jessy, can you teach me to play 'Simon Says'?"

"Yes Mommy, but I don't have any treats to give you unless you want the rest of my orange juice. It wouldn't be fair if I didn't give you anything."

"Okay Jessy, this time you'll just be teaching me, and next time you can give me a treat. How about that?"

"Okay Mommy, if you don't want your treat don't be mad at me. Are you ready, Mommy?"

"Yes, I'm ready."

"Mommy, if Simon doesn't say it, you don't do it, okay? If you do, you're going to be out and you won't get a treat. Are you ready?"

"Yes, Jessy."

"Okay. Get ready, get set, and go. Take off your shoes."

I started taking off my shoes just to see if Jessy really knew what she was doing.

"No, no, Mommy. Simon didn't say it. I'm going to give you one more chance. *Simon says* take off your shirt and your pants."

By this time, Dr. Bradshaw and the nurse were knocking on the door and asking if they could come in. Dr. Bradshaw asked if he could speak with me for just a minute outside the door while the nurse accompanied Jessy.

"Mrs. Taylor?"

"Yes."

"As you know, there's a mirror in Jessy's room as well as an intercom. We could see and hear you on the other side. Mrs. Foster wanted to see how Jessy interacted with you. We've recorded and taped what just happened. I can't believe a man would allow a child to call him 'Grandpa' then manipulate her into sexual encounters with him. I've already examined Jessy and the other child. They've been through the same trauma. The only difference is Amber has been penetrated with something larger than Jessy."

"What do you mean, Dr. Bradshaw?"

"In other words, there's something located on the entrance of the vaginal area called a hymen. When this layer of skin has been broken, that is an indication of interference in that area."

"How could you tell if there is major or minor tampering?"

"To be clear with you, Mrs. Taylor, Jessy has been penetrated with something the size of a finger, considering the condition of her vaginal area. And Amber has been penetrated with something the size of a man's penis. Amber's mom gave me permission to discuss the nature of her daughter's case with you. She said if it weren't for your suspicion in the way your daughter acted with her dolls, she doesn't know how long it would've taken her to find out something was wrong with Amber. You were a very smart woman, Mrs. Taylor, to take action the way you did."

"Where's Helen? I wanna speak with her."

"We had to give her a sedative to calm her down. She's in denial and a state of shock at the moment. We've placed her in a room until she gets herself together. We've also taken Amber down to the nursery. I've seen many cases come through these doors, but never have I ever seen any children as calm as these two. From the information I have gathered from Amber, this man has played 'Simon Says' with all the children at once.

"Mrs. Charles has given us all the information we need on Mr. Dickerson. The investigating officer is getting an arrest warrant from the judge as we speak to apprehend this man."

"Oh, Lord Jesus, thank you, thank you so much. I don't know how I let this happen, and I don't know what I'm going to do to make it better for Jessy."

"Mrs. Taylor, there's a lot that has to be done. This is just the beginning. We're going to check Jessy out again and then we're going to set up an appointment with a family counselor that deals with these types of cases."

"Okay, anything . . . I'm willing to do anything for Jessy."

The examination the doctor performed on Jessy coupled with the conversation that followed was the hardest time of my life. After the news got out and Mr. Dickerson, AKA Grandpa, was exploited for his sexual abuse, people that lived in the neighborhood started getting their children evaluated to see if he'd tampered with them, too. About twenty to twenty-five kids were sexually abused by the masked man they knew as Grandpa.

He manipulated those children with everything he thought they loved or wanted to get them to do exactly what he wanted and to keep it a secret. He led them to believe everything was normal. By them not showing any signs of abuse, he ended up hiding behind his mask for years. I could only imagine how many other innocent children Mr. Dickerson hurt on his journey to sixty-three—almost sixty-four years old.

Thank God, Mr. Dickerson didn't want to sit there listening to each and every child talk about what 'Grandpa' did as they pointed to him in court. After the second child came forward, he told his lawyer that he was willing to plead out to twenty years in prison, which was his original offer. He'll be eighty-three years old before he can put his mask on again.

Chapter 7

(Poetic Pain)

I'm a mother who carries my daughter's pain,
But then again it's my own pain.
The agony of being blind to the unknown,
Especially when the circumstances surround my own home
We can't work and be with our children twenty-four hours a day,
But we can sit and listen to what they say.
Never judge a book by its cover.
Sometimes it'll take you up;
sometimes it'll take you down.
It'll even end up making you look like the clown.
Always allow one's charm to make you wonder
how much evil they may ponder down under.
I'm a mother who didn't pay enough attention.
Now my child is being rehabilitated from a condition that she was too afraid to mention.

Dorothy Hall

Comments on Chapter 7:

In chapter seven, a mother explains how embarrassed she was to speak out about the sexual molestation that took place right beneath her nose. Of course, we never intend for this to happen to our children. That's why it's always a must to know that you can never be too careful.

Now the woman is thinking back to the time she thought her job was more important than securing the safety of her child. I know this woman was ashamed because she'd been terribly humiliated. So what! Her humiliation wasn't worse than what her daughter suffered with a man she trusted with her everything. When a child thinks of Grandpa, he is supposed to light up a child's life like the stars light up the sky at night.

Instead, this man brought a reign of terror. Did she really know Grandpa? No, of course not. She was new in the neighborhood and immediately took a liking to this man because everyone else had him on a pedestal.

The masked molester sits back patiently as they hunt their prey. No need to hurry, because they want to be sure that no harm can come to them if any foul play is suspiciously pointed in their direction. They'll charm you. They'll cry out to you, as if you're doing something wrong when you accuse them. They'll try to make you feel sorry for them to evade what's really going on.

Don't be manipulated by the masked molester. Proceed to take action to get to the bottom of the situation.

Chapter 8

Uncle Jerry Taught Me to Drive

My name is Button.

Today is my lucky day! Uncle Jerry is gonna teach me to drive. He told me if I made all A's on this six week report card, he'll take me out for hot Krispy Kreme doughnuts and milk that I love so much. Really, I'm too young to drive, but Uncle Jerry says it doesn't matter and that I'll just be ahead of the other girls my age. Uncle Jerry says I'm more mature than other girls, and I'm becoming a beautiful young lady. I love my uncle Jerry so much. He's like a dad to me. My biological father passed away when my mom was six months pregnant with me. I've seen pictures of my dad, and he looks just like Uncle Jerry, who's six-feet tall and has big muscles. Everybody loves him.

I hear a car pulling up, and it sounds like Uncle Jerry. It is Uncle Jerry!

"Hi Uncle Jerry, I've been waiting on you. You're ten minutes late," I said.

"Uncle Jerry is sorry, baby. Are you ready to go?" he asked.

"Yes, I'm ready. I told you I've been waiting."

"Where's your report card? I need to see it first."

"Okay, I'll go get it." I turned to exit the room.

"Don't forget to tell your mom we're leaving?" Uncle Jerry said, stopping me in my tracks.

"She's asleep, so I'll leave her a note beside her bed."

"Make sure you do that."

I ran to my room to get my report card and I wrote a quick note to my mother telling her I was with Uncle Jerry. Five minutes later, I was standing in front of Uncle Jerry with the report card in my hand.

"Here's my report card. All A's like I told you."

"That's my girl, Button. Your dad would be very proud of you. Give Uncle Jerry a kiss and a big hug." I gave him a kiss and a big hug as he insisted.

Once we got to the donut place, we went in to sit down. Uncle Jerry would usually leave me in the car, pick up the donuts and we'd leave. I knew he was very proud of my report card. He actually took the time to sit and eat donuts with me. He's always a very busy man. His cell phone rings all day and he's always talking. I admire him so much. "Uncle Jerry, are you gonna answer that phone? It keeps ringing."

"No, as a matter of fact, I'm turning it off. Today is your day." Uncle Jerry and I ate. We talked, we laughed, and he washed the milk from around my mouth. He made me feel so special.

After we were done with the donuts, Uncle Jerry said, "Are you ready to drive now?"

"Oh yes, Uncle Jerry. I thought you were kidding about that part."

"If you don't wanna go, you don't have to."

"Yes, yes, I wanna go. I just thought you were pulling my leg."

"What do you know about somebody pulling your leg?"

"I heard Momma and her friends say it."

Masked Molestation

"Quit repeating everything you hear. It gets you in trouble. Let's go."

Uncle Jerry and I were driving for about forty-five minutes and I could tell we were outside of our district, because I'd never seen the things I was seeing before.

"Button, we'll be there in five more minutes."

"Okay, Uncle Jerry. No rush for me."

Finally, Uncle Jerry turned onto a dirt road, and all I could see was red dirt ahead and big tall trees on both sides.

Uncle Jerry reached over and rubbed my leg. I didn't think anything at first. Then his hand went farther up my dress and I began to feel uncomfortable because I knew it was wrong. Uncle Jerry pulled over to the side. With the car still running, he put it in park and moved the seat back. He told me to climb across onto his lap so he could teach me how to guide the steering wheel first. I obeyed and did like Uncle Jerry told me to do.

I climbed onto his lap, placing my hands around the steering wheel. Uncle Jerry put the car in drive and pressed the accelerator slightly as he guided me in steering the wheel. I could feel something hard against my bottom. Uncle Jerry grabbed me around the waist, positioning me on his lap. Then he started to run his hand up my dress, while telling me to pay attention to the road. I started to panic, and then I started screaming.

Uncle Jerry got angry. "Button, you stop that screaming right now! I thought you wanted me to teach you to drive." I never said anything. I just sat there shaking and crying.

Uncle Jerry stopped the car and opened the door. He said, "Get off my lap and walk around to the other side."

I got out of the car and walked around to the other side. Before I could get my hand on the door handle good, he pulled off, leaving me in the middle of nowhere. There were no cars coming nor anyone. It seemed as though I was all alone. When nighttime came, I could hear the sounds of nature so clearly in my ears. I didn't know if something would come bursting through the trees to get me or what. I didn't have a watch, but I could tell it had been several hours since Uncle Jerry left me out there. Suddenly, I saw headlights from a car. I was sticking out my hand and jumping up and down hoping to be seen. The only bad part was that it was Uncle Jerry.

"Get in, Button. Your momma is gonna be worried sick about you. I can't believe you got out of the car and refused to get back in," he said.

"I don't wanna get in."

"Well, you only have two choices. Either get in the car with me and be safe, or stay out here where something is bound to get you and kill you. I'll tell your momma I brought you back home hours ago and act like everything is normal."

I took a look around me and thought twice. I had no choice but to get in the car. As soon as I got in, he pulled my dress up and ripped my panties. He said, "Listen to me, little girl. Don't you ever disrespect me like that again after I've been so good to you!"

All I could do was cry and say, "Yes, sir, I won't do it again."

"I know you won't, because if you do I'll kill you and your mother. Get in the back seat, now! If you breathe a word to anyone, I promise you some people are gonna be found dead. Do you hear me, little girl?"

"Yes sir."

"Now lay down and you better not move."

That day Uncle Jerry hurt me really bad. I never told anyone because I was too afraid of what he might do. The tragedy of it all was having to look in his face every single day and call him Uncle Jerry, hoping that wasn't the day he decided to take me for more driving lessons.

Till this day, Uncle Jerry is a very well respected business man whom everyone loves. To my knowledge, I am the only one who knows that he wears a mask.

Comments on Chapter 8:

Manipulation plays a major role in sexual molestation. The masked molester plays every card he has until he/she finds their trump card.

Here in chapter eight, the masked molester begins his manipulation by doting on the child's education and continues on down to her dead father being proud of her if he were still alive.

What a cruel way to reel in a child. Now, is this child ever going to learn to trust again, and when she does how long will it take? Nine times out of ten when she has her own children, if ever, she'll be so overprotective the child won't be able to breathe nor have a chance to live life for himself until the mother realizes she's not living her life through this child all over again.

Uncle Jerry, a man that looks exactly like her dead father, probably made a question run through her mind about her own dad if he were alive. She probably asked herself, "Would my dad have treated me like this?" Or, "Would he have protected me?" There are so many things that could've been going through Button's mind when Uncle Jerry left her out in the middle of nowhere on a deserted dirt road.

The masked molester took her out of her comfort zone to scare her into doing what he wanted her to do and keep quiet about it. The entire setup was a premeditated manipulation of a sexual predator seeking his prey, waiting to strike again and proceeding without caution.

CHAPTER 9

MISGUIDED DIVORCE

My mom and dad were high school sweethearts. Just after graduation they were married. Mom was pregnant with me. Three years later, my brother was born.

We moved frequently to different states due to my father's line of work. To me, my parents seemed to be happy, although it didn't turn out that way. My father left when my brother turned six years old. Three years later, my mom decided to let us go spend the summer with our father. I was twelve at the time. The divorce was final. Mom had no reason to be worried. With Mom being on the east coast and my dad on the west coast, Dad had the upper hand. He stabbed Mom in the back by tricking me into writing a letter to the judge that stated that I wanted to reside with him. I didn't know it would be permanent. Dad filed for custody. Mom had no financial income that would allow her to fly back and forth for these court proceedings. My dad won primary custody of us from my mother on the grounds of abandonment and a lack of financial support to care for my brother and me.

My father was an ex-military and he treated us accordingly. He'd give us severe spankings and punishments whenever we did something wrong.

Time passed and I guess my dad was lonely for the companionship of a woman. First, he made me do the cooking and cleaning. It seemed like I was taking on the role of what my mother used to do. I couldn't go anywhere, nor could I have any friends over to visit.

One Saturday night, I was up watching a blockbuster movie. My dad came in late from work. I placed his plate in the microwave as he'd instructed me to do early on. After finishing his dinner, my father came over to join me while watching the movie. This night wasn't our usual night for watching a movie together. My brother was fast asleep, and Dad seemed to be really relaxed. In the middle of the movie, he began to remove his clothing. Looking at him out the corner of my eyes, I wondered what in the world was he doing. He got butt naked and sat down on the couch beside me, stroking his penis. I moved toward the opposite end of the couch, and as I moved over, he came closer. Dad grabbed my hand and told me to touch his penis.

I said, "No."

He responded, "Don't you ever tell your father no. I'm the one that gave you life in your mother's womb." I stroked his penis and then he said, "Kiss it for Daddy." Tears rolled down my face as I leaned over to kiss my father's penis. He pulled my shirt over my head, leaving me bare chested. My father made me sit there and kiss his penis until he was satisfied. That one night led to many similar nights and ones even worse throughout the next four years.

When he started molesting me, the spankings stopped, but they continued for my brother. My dad is my brother's whole world. I never wanted my little brother to know the horrible things our father had been doing to me. So I kept quiet.

Masked Molestation

Now it has been several years and dad is now a police officer. I've heard stories about him having young girls over to his house, and the parents making accusations. All I can do now is wonder if he has reeled in another innocent child while hiding behind his mask.

Dorothy Hall

Comments on Chapter 9:

A child who hasn't fully gone through puberty is forced to take on the world and portray the role of a grown woman.

Due to misguided divorce, the father here in chapter nine went from physically abusing the children to sexually abusing his daughter. He never wanted the children. He only wanted to punish the mother and used the children to do so.

It shouldn't matter who has the most money to financially take care of a child, just as long as they are able to receive the things they need. Needing and wanting fall into two different categories. The facts should be considered as to where the safety of the child is guaranteed.

This young woman has built walls that a bulldozer would have trouble knocking down. She has trouble trusting in relationships, and when she does, the least little thing can trigger her to act outside of her character. She wanted to confront her father, and she did so by searching for answers and closure.

Confronting him by mail and receiving consecutive responses of apologies gave her some peace, although she hasn't forgotten. But she needed to do something so she could carry on with her life. She wrote letters and felt that this was the easiest way for her to get a breakthrough. She just prays he's retired as a masked man, so she won't be sorry for protecting her brother's image of the good father at the expense of another child.

Chapter 10

A Letter to the People Who've Hurt Me

When I was a child, you robbed me of my childhood and don't get me wrong, as there's nothing I would do to go back and change it. It made me the woman I am today, even though I still have some of the baggage you bestowed upon me when you stole my innocence. But one day at a time, I am healing and learning to release it. I didn't write this letter to only the person reading it. There are multiple letters the same as this one given to multiple people. I don't have to tell you each what you've done to me, because you know your role in bringing havoc to my life.

The good thing now is that I forgive you because my heart can't allow me not to.

Ephesians 4:32: "And be kind to one another, tenderhearted, forgiving one another even as God in Christ forgave you."

Who am I not to forgive when God forgave me? The thing I worry about the most is: Can you take responsibility for your actions when asking God to forgive you? How long is it going take you to forgive yourself for what you've taken away from an innocent child?

God bless your soul.

Comments on Chapter Ten:

Chapter ten exposes the feelings of a woman who's a victim of sexual molestation who has used her life's struggles as stepping stones.

She feels that all she's endured has given her a different perspective in life. She explains that the healing process isn't going to happen overnight. But she's taking it one day at a time and releasing it accordingly.

She speaks out through this letter to her masked molesters to lift the weight of not being able to forgive for so many years. It has had her in a mental bondage that she no longer wants to be in.

Her closing remarks state her forgiveness and the question to the masked molesters about asking God to forgive them. That's heavy, but so true. The woman has gone through enough and has had enough taken away. She wasn't about to let her hatred out of pain keep her from walking through the gates of heaven.

She had to let go and let God.

Chapter 11
Never Degrade Your Child

Even though people most likely never intend to degrade their child or hurt their pride, so to speak, it still often happens. Let me give you my opinion and a hypothetical scenario of what can happen.

Suppose you've had a bad day at work. Coming home in a horrible state of mind, you find clothing in the laundry all thrown together. The first thing that comes to your mind is, I've told Terry a hundred times whites go in the white basket and colored in the opposite basket.

It's not even about the children. It's about a bad day you encountered at work, and not giving yourself ample time to cool down. You lash out at anything that gets under your skin. This particular day, the colored clothes are sticking out like a sore thumb and this adds more fuel to the fire.

There's a knock at the door. It's Liz. Why not lash out at her? Instead, you invite her in, being very courteous and saying, "Hello Liz, come in and take a load off. Is there anything I can get you?"

"No thank you, I'm fine at the moment," Liz says as she takes a seat across from you.

"Girl, I had a bad day at the job."

"What happened?"

"One of my co-workers didn't show up for work today. Therefore, I had an overload causing me to miss out on other engagements. I'm so frustrated!"

"Can you reschedule the appointments you missed?"

"Yes, but that's not the point. I hate being late; that doesn't show good ethics at all."

Then, your son Terry comes walking through the house with his headphones on. "Hi Mom," he says with a smile on his face.

In a high-pitched angry voice, you respond, "Don't 'hi mom' me. Who put those colored clothes in with the whites?"

"I don't know. It wasn't me. Maybe it was Amy."

"You're always putting something on Amy. If you did it, you better tell the truth and I mean right now. That's why I never believe anything you say."

Liz is sitting there observing everything that's going on, and Terry's feelings are extremely hurt. Liz's being there makes it worse on Terry.

Then Amy comes strolling in the door and says, "Hi, Mom."

"Amy, did you mix the colored clothes with the whites today?"

"Oh, yes Mom. I'm sorry. I was in a rush for dance practice. I'll get them out now."

Terry storms out the door, mad. You didn't even bother to tell him you're sorry for not believing him.

Yes, kids do tend to misguide us sometimes. That doesn't mean you're to degrade them in front of company. Next thing you know, Terry doesn't show up on time for dinner. He knows dinner is at 6:30 p.m. and everyone eats together. You're worried and out looking for him. The masked molester has once again invaded on your child's innocence.

The mask molester uses that as her weapon. She's drawn him in because of his vulnerability at the moment, and she's able to manipulate him to do whatever she wants him to do. She also reminds him that his mother doesn't trust one word that comes out of his mouth. The child is then scorned for life because you gave the masked molester power over your child.

Did you know Liz was capable of molesting a child? No, of course you didn't. But that's just the thing. All Liz had to do was observe the child's surroundings and relationship with the parent before attacking.

A few things I've learned about anger:

- Tune into what is going on in your body and decide what happened to make you feel that way.

    A. Take a step back, a moment to calm down before dealing with anything else, especially your child.

- Understand other's feelings, the child's feelings.

    A. Watch the child's reaction.
    B. Listen to what the child is saying before you jump to conclusions.
    C. Figure out what the child may be feeling.
    D. Think about ways to show you understand what the child is feeling.

Chapter 12

Searching for Daylight

In the dark for so many years, I long for daylight. In the physical I can see, but in my mind and my heart I can't find a path to a place called home. I am surrounded by the people who are supposed to protect me, but they leave me on a path of darkness without a compass and unable to see. What am I to do? I know the people around me can see, but they choose not to open their eyes to what's going on with me. Do they intend for me to sit in darkness my entire life because they want to protect their image as people? Or, are they just too head over heels in love that they don't wanna face the truth of the misery standing before them? Is not the love of a child more sacred than the love of a man or woman who's deceived the child and stolen something sacred from them? Is it not more important to protect the innocence of a child than keep someone in your life that means you more harm than good? Shame on those of you that do.

Open the door. Let the daylight shine in and snatch the mask off the molester.

Chapter 13

A Pretty Picture

The masked molester paints a pretty picture, but behind closed doors nobody knows the extent of this pain he's caused me to endure.

This man has a mask well painted on his face that nobody can see. He's like the devil, out to steal, kill and destroy. The innocence of a child doesn't matter to him. He only cares about his selfish, sick, sexual desires. He brings a reign of terror on the helpless, and then abandons them with the pain of his actions. He's cruel, self-seeking and doesn't discriminate on any sexual preference or culture. He's a mean annihilating machine, able to assassinate the character of the immature in their own minds. The masked molester is a sick individual clearly conscious of the actions carried out in his head.

Just as a premeditated murderer knows his victims beforehand, so does the masked molester. The only difference is the person murdered no longer suffers, but the person molested still endures until he or she finds an outlet or a sense of peace within to overcome the misery of their masked molester.

Chapter 14

Almost Suffocated

The child that lives within me still tries to catch her breath when she thinks of all the times she was a victim of sexual molestation. For years I've thought to myself, Why me? What did I do to deserve this? Why did I get picked at random to be a victim of such heinous acts? I guess somebody had to be chosen in order to shine the light on masked molesters, so people could see the damage caused by sexual abuse. Not to mention the mental abuse, which can be more detrimental depending on how the child may cope with the abuse. Not everybody that's a victim of sexual abuse deals with it in the same manner. Just like somebody being shot, one person may be left with a limp; the other may walk away with the scar left from the bullet or even lose their life.

For years I kept my issues to myself. I thought, *What was the use? I didn't tell anybody back then, so why now?* It wasn't the point of telling someone now to get justice on the person that invaded my body. It was about getting justice for me. I needed an outlet.

If I'd kept it inside any longer, it might have destroyed me. It might have been my reasons for shutting the people out that I needed most. It was the reason I was afraid to get close to anyone because of a lack of trust. I thought, *they too would find my weakness and try to use it against me to their advantage.* When I was eight, my weakness was the love I had for my father and the unconditional love he had

Masked Molestation

for me. Every little girl dreams of a father like mine. In my eyes, he was a man always there to catch me when I fall, a man that put me first in his life. My dad is all those things. He made his mistakes in life, but never did he once violate me.

We had an intruder that manipulated my father into thinking she loved him. Then she manipulated me to think my father would turn against me if I told him one thing and she told him another. She was a true master of disguise when it came to my father.

At eight years old it's hard to dissect what's standing right in front of your face. Now that I'm older, I know to believe half of what I see. Back then, what appeared to be two people in love was really the opposite of what I thought. It was only a fantasy. How could I come to my father and say, "Your girlfriend has been doing uncomfortable things to me. She told me if I tell you, you'd believe her and not me. She also said she'd tell you I've been a bad girl, and I've been messing with one of the little boys in the neighborhood. But that's not true. I promise you, it's not true. I would never do anything to disappoint you. I want you to make her stop. Put her out of our house. Show me that you believe me and not her." Those were the things I practiced saying to myself in the mirror every morning before I went to school and every night before I went to bed.

I never built up the nerve to say anything. She had me terrified to confide in my own father. What hurt me the most was the pressure of having to go along with her sick little games. Then it got worse. She'd say, "If you don't start coming to me, I guess I'm gonna have to tell your father you've been doing some very naughty things behind his back."

Now, here's a woman, *not* a man, violating a little girl. For what reason, I didn't know. Even to this day I have no clue why a woman would do this to a little girl. Women are supposed to be the mothers of all living things; it's in their nature. It makes me wonder beyond the point of my being sexually abused: What was she getting out of this? Did I do something to make her think I wanted her to treat me this way? Did my dad have sucker written across his forehead? Did this come down from another generation? Was it a curse on my family from many years ago? All of these questions came to mind, but would we ever find out the real truth behind all of this besides her being sick in the head? Excuses aren't allowed. We need some serious answers. We need an antidote if it's a sickness. Let's cure the disease.

After being introduced to sexual abuse for the first time, it seemed like people, other masked molesters, were waiting in line like they were at a local convenience store. It was like a come one, come all. The only difference was everybody came with a different purchase.

Persuasion and manipulation were their winning poker hand. Of course, their hands would trump that of an eight year old because she never knew how to play the game. She had never played before. They put the cards in her hand and taught her how to play to their advantage.

Strangely, after going through all that I've gone through, people would've thought I'd have a nervous breakdown and need to be put in a mental institution. Like I explained before, all people cope with the unexpected in life differently. I was one of the children who chose to take life into my own hands. I didn't have a clue where I would end up in life. I just live one day at a time. To be honest, I took what I learned from my abusers and started manipulating the circumstances around me in order to make it another day without having to go back home. It was like survival of the fittest for me. Only if I had known differently, maybe I would have stopped to think: Should I tell and take my chances?

Today, very seldom do you see things on TV that teaches a child to tell if there's been foul play. It's not enough. Parents, caretakers, and the most influential people in the world that care about what happens to the children of our future should lend a hand in making these things known to children. I feel schools should even touch on the subject enough to let the children know what can happen just in case they do come face to face with a situation like this. Just like they teach sex education and teen pregnancy, they should address this issue. Not every parent/caretaker would agree with me, but why not? Do they have something to hide? Educating students about sexual abuse would also help to minimize these malicious acts. The children would be aware when they are approached. It's always nice to have your gun cocked and ready when an intruder invades your space. It's like knowing who God is. If the devil approaches you and you don't know scripture to protect yourself, the enemy is able to step inside your bubble and do as he pleases, or manipulate you into doing what he wants you to do. Just like the devil approaches you in many disguises, so does the masked molesters.

Take my situation for instance. The woman appeared to love me so much in my father's eyes, and then she turned and used that against me to her advantage. When people came over to our home, they were impressed with how well she was taking care of another woman's child. A pretty picture was what she painted for them. What adults don't know is the secret lies within the child. Sometimes children have a lot more to say than adults give them credit for. Only if adults would take the time out to listen, they'd learn that the child has more to say than they are ready to hear. If only parents would stop and give that extra few minutes out of the day to pay closer attention to their children, the world would be a better place as far as this subject is concerned. Parents that think they are doing everything they could possibly do for their children tend to neglect what's really needed in their child's life. That conversation at night and the bond of honesty and trust will make a difference. Sometimes the child needs a little reassuring that the parent is there for them.

In between the times of a parent having an intimate talk with the child, there may have been an intruder to come in and assassinate everything positive they've shared and replaced that parent-child conversation with negative things. It's called word play. They would tell them almost the same thing the parent told them, but put a little spin on it so they can have the ball in their court. Now to the child, the ball is being juggled back and forth, and they don't know who to believe.

Masked Molestation

Reinforcement with the child is a major asset to protecting your child from the manipulation of the intruder.

I've had more heartache and pain in the streets than I could have ever imagined, but it taught me how to love and become a better person. Still, I don't wish what I went through in the streets on any child. I'm still going through the growing pains. One thing I can say about that is it gets better as each day passes. Being able to sit here and complete this book is another part of my healing process. Knowing it will help others gives me joy and contentment in my heart.

A dear friend of mine shared her story with me. The only difference between the two of us is that it was her father. This young lady has so much love in her heart, I can't understand it. She's so forgiving until it hurts, but at the same time she looks for love in all the wrong places. I'm at the place where I'm unable to trust anyone; she's the complete opposite. She's open to giving everyone the benefit of the doubt. I feel it's because she could never imagine anyone else doing the things to her that her father did. Even though she's been let down time and time again, she still sets herself up for one disappointment after another. At this point in my life, I couldn't imagine letting someone into my space so easily. I've learned how to live and let go because that's the only way I'm going to be able to live a normal life. Still, I'm particular with my surroundings. Forgiving doesn't mean you have to forget. It's smart to always take the lessons with you that you've learned in life. It may help the next person.

Dorothy Hall

Before now, I was bitter inside out, even when it didn't show. The mind and the heart are terrible things to waste. Being a victim of such acts takes a major toll on some people's lives. They are unable to live a normal healthy life if they can't find a way to cope and put that chapter of their lives behind them and press toward the future. Some people will need counseling and guidance, so they won't be subjected to taking justice into their own hands. Some people look for the satisfaction of being in control; this way they can control what they allow to hurt them. Others have killed in order to satisfy the thirst of wanting justice for what happened to them. Murder definitely isn't the answer. The victim may not be thinking rationally, depending on their state of mind at that moment in their life. In a situation of this nature, everybody loses. I'm hoping for a solution to minimize, if not end, what seems to be turning into an epidemic. Sexual molestation doesn't need to disrupt the minds of any more children and navigate its way into another generation.

In the beginning when the woman invaded my space, I was caught off guard. While she was violating my body, I was told to put a pillow over my face so I couldn't witness with the naked eye what she was doing to me. I may not have had a name to call what she was doing to me, but I knew it was a violation of my body. With the pillow covering my face and body, my mind and soul were being violated. I almost suffocated, but I found a breakthrough. Will the next child be so blessed to bloom into a fully grown woman/man and find their breakthrough? Will they suffocate within themselves, living as a prisoner trapped inside their own body? Or will they find a way to get rid of the anger, hostility, resentment and the recurring thought of the violation itself?

By the grace of God I pray that every family that's been a victim of sexual abuse has that one person with broad courage who's able to put the spotlight on the masked molester, so the world can see what lies beneath the mask.

Chapter 15

Don't Bond So Quickly With Strangers Around Your Children

Imagine being out at the grocery store with your child. You drop something. A stranger (but not really a stranger because you've seen him/her around before), immediately comes over to help you retrieve the item from the floor. Before I go any further, let me say that some people have good intentions, but some have cruel intentions, so be cautious of the ones who mean you no good.

You two begin to have a mutual conversation, laughing and talking. You really don't know this person, though. There's your child standing there registering all this information from your small talk. In turn, the person uses this to their advantage.

Two weeks later, Brianna is walking home from school and you're running late from work. She has her umbrella and raincoat, and she's walking up the sidewalk. The masked molester is on the prowl, looking for another victim. Bam! He sees Brianna walking along the sidewalk minding her own business. He then slows down and says, "Hi Brianna, I'm your mom's friend. Remember you met me at the grocery store?"

"Yes," she replies as she stops to be respectful.

"Come on. I'm gonna give you a ride home."

"No thank you. My mommy told me not to take any rides."

"But it's okay. Here, I'll call her on her cell to see if it's okay with her." He picks up the phone, dials an imaginary number, acting as if he's having a conversation with mom.

"Hello Janice, its Brad. I'm here with Brianna and I want to give her a ride home. She says you wouldn't like it if she took a ride with me." Now he starts to act as if he's responding to someone on the other end. "Okay, okay, I'll let her know. Yes, we'll be there in about ten minutes." He hangs up the phone.

"What did Mommy say?" Brianna asks.

"She said it'll be fine, and she will meet us there in ten minutes."

Brianna gets in the car and the ten minutes turn into an hour. He never bothers to bring Brianna home. After he has his way with her and threatens to kill her if she tells anyone, he drops her off at the very same spot he picked her up, so she can walk home and come up with her own explanation for being late.

How many years will Brianna have to live with this, just because she thought Brad was a family friend?

Just when we think our children know better, the people who commit these malicious actions manipulate our children into their webs to tear their innocence away from them.

CHAPTER 16

PAYING ATTENTION TO YOUR CHILDREN

Always pay close attention to your children to see if there's a change in their behavior. Look for signs. Some children tend to associate what they are enduring or have endured with the things around them. For instance, if a child has been sexually abused by someone and it only takes place at nighttime, when nighttime comes you will see a change in the child's behavior. They will be terrified, or they may even ask you questions they've never asked before that may seem strange to you.

Others may wet the bed in the middle of a beautiful day outside, when this isn't something they usually do. Why? Because the parents usually aren't home in the daytime. They're out working and this is the time the predator starts to hunt their prey.

Maybe the child hasn't seen the predator for a couple of days. Then daddy walks into your home wearing cologne that the molester, Uncle Jerry, wore three days ago. The smell will trigger the child's memory, and by the child being so afraid and scared to tell anyone, they'll wet their clothes where they stand.

Just think of that little person standing there unable to protect themselves. What would you do? They are so terrified. Only God knows what the masked molester has told them in order to keep them quiet.

Don't always assume the negative about your child. All children will respond differently as a result of being victims of sexual abuse. Parents tend to think the child is only acting out because they're seeking attention or they want things to go their way, not knowing what's really going on. In some cases this will happen, but not in all cases.

Take a child that's lacking attention in the home. A predator, AKA masked molester, will use that to their advantage to reel the child in under cruel attentions. Then the masked molester will proceed to fill your space as a parent, catering to the child's every need and hoping to create a relationship by allowing the child to put all their trust in them. Once this mission is accomplished, the shark attacks.

The masked molester would've already planted seeds in the child's head and began to water them using the weakness from a lack of attention by the primary caretaker as the tool.

The masked molester will tell the child numerous things, such as:

1. "Your parents don't have time for you."

2. "Eventually they'll send you off to a foster home, boarding school, or with other relatives that don't want you."

3. "If you tell them anything about our secret, I'll deny it. And they won't believe anything you say because you're a spoiled, rotten little brat that wants everything to go your way."

CHAPTER 17

FACTS

These days, many children are sexually molested. I've encountered many women who are victims of sexual molestation and are still afraid to confront their masked molester. They've walked around with this shame concealed for years, unable to speak about this without falling apart all over again.

It's not that they can't get past the tragedy. It's just the point of taking the initiative, that first step to get help or talk to someone willing to help them get on with their lives.

Some people are very judgmental when it comes to something of this nature. Why? Because they haven't experienced it themselves. All victims of molestation are tragedies, but some may be far worse than others, depending upon the way the act was carried out. But molestation in any form leaves the same scar.

Some victims were inside homes where the family wants to keep quiet. Some were taken from their homes and dared to tell. If so, they were told it would result in the death of someone they loved. Others slept at a friend's home during a slumber party, only to be awakened in the wee hours of the night to face their masked molester.

I chose the title **Masked Molestation** for this book, because these molesters were never apprehended for their actions. There are still men and women today who have their mask on. We need to recognize this and have them called accordingly to pay for the crimes they've committed.

Masked Molestation

Snatch the mask off and let them be seen for the predators they are. Don't protect them. If you are going to be biased about this situation, put it into someone's hand who is not, so it can be handled in a manner where only the facts are considered.

Chapter 18

Scorned by the Devil's Advocates

Every page in this book entails the truth about the devil's advocates. All of the victims were scorned by the same sword, but by different degrees of heinous actions.

After reading this book based on true stories, I pray that you grasp the concept of what's going on here and the depth of the pain caused. Detestable actions such as these by the masked molesters that may be living next door to us, working for or with us, or who may be a member of our family, or just a simple stranger we could happen to meet in a grocery store, can cause more damage than we could ever imagine.

You can never be too careful, and nobody is perfect. You can't watch your child every second of the day. But you *can* build that trusting bond with them, allowing them to trust that they can be open and honest with you about any and everything.

A close-knit relationship with your child can make a tremendous difference in the way they'll react to someone mistreating them or touching them in a way they shouldn't be touched.

Don't allow the devil to come into your life to destroy and steal away the innocence of your child.

Chapter 19

Seeking Help for a Breakthrough

Whether your problem is being the victim of sexual molestation, or being the caretaker of someone who has been sexually molested, all of the aforementioned puts a strain on you to some degree.

Most people are embarrassed about the situation and circumstances surrounding the strike by a sexual molester. There's no need to be embarrassed to get help. You'll find that there are many people in this world dealing with the same thing you're dealing with, and who are unable to discuss it based on the feelings of shame, as though they've done something wrong.

Don't feel embarrassed or ashamed. Seek the help you need to cope with the storm that's entered your life. After taking the initiative to seek help, you will find other individuals in group therapy sitting there quietly, introverted, looking as though there's nothing going on with them. Then the question comes to your mind: Why is he/she here? Simple answer: Because they need help tackling a similar situation, if not worse.

It's common for most people to think they are in an awkward situation all alone. That's not true. You can't even start to imagine how many more people have walked in the same shoes.

In group settings, some people are willing to freely open up right away while others are reluctant to do so at first, worrying if they are going to be judged. They may need someone to help them open up with what they have buried deep down inside for only God knows how long.

Once they have found comfort in the group, they will start to release a little at a time. By the time the entire session is over, they will be thanking the chief in the group. I use the term 'chief' to mean leadership. Someone has to take that first step. If that person is you, my hat goes off to you, because you would be that person to help open healing doors for others. Where the chief goes, the Indians are sure to follow. This step opens the first door, allowing others into a state of ease and contentment within the group.

We need the strong to guide us and to pass the strength along to us. This will move us in the direction to free us from the bondage of suffering consecutively with the pain that follows after a masked molester has invaded our territory.

An inspirational insert taken from the Holy Bible "Woman Thou Art Loosed" Edition by T.D. Jakes:

The Covering (Psalm 91:1-13):

In the process of creating Eve, the mother of all living, God's timing was crucial. He did not unveil her until everything she needed was provided. From establishment to relationship, all things were in order. Woman was meant to be covered, to be nurtured and protected. Originally, Adam was her covering. My sister, even as a child, you were made to be covered. If someone "uncovered" you, there is a feeling of being violated. Even when these feelings are suppressed, they are still powerful. I think it is interesting that when the Bible talks about incest, it uses the word uncovered. Sexual abuse violates the covering of the family and the responsible person whom you looked to for guidance. This stripping away of relationships leaves you exposed and vulnerable to the reality of corrupt, lustful imaginations. Like fruit peeled too soon, it is wrong to uncover what God wished to remain protected.

To molest a child is to uncover her, to leave her feeling unprotected. Do you realize that one of the things the blood of Jesus Christ does is to cover us? Like Noah's sons, Japheth and Shem, who covered their father's nakedness, the blood of Jesus will cover the uncovered. He will not allow you to spend the rest of your life exposed and violated. For the wounded and hurting, God has intensive care. There may be times in your life when God nurtures you through a crisis. On the other hand, you may not even realize the many times he intervenes to relieve the tensions and stresses of everyday living. He knows when the load is overwhelming. And he moves just in the nick of time.

The Bible instructs husbands to dwell with their wives according to knowledge and understanding (1 Peter 3:7). It will pay every husband to understand that many women do not deal easily with such stress as unpaid bills and financial disorder. A feeling of security is a plus in matters of the home. That same principle is just as important when it comes to your relationship with the Lord. He is constantly reassuring you that you have a consolation and a hope for your soul.

Reach out and embrace the fact that God has been watching over you all your life. My sister, he covers you, clothes you, and blesses you. Rejoice in him in spite of the broken places. God's grace is sufficient for your needs and your scars. He will anoint you with oil. The anointing of the Lord be upon you now!

Chapter 20

Resolving the Issues

The information I am sharing in this chapter will help those that are hurting because of a masked molester. Hopefully, some or all of this information with enable you or someone else to resolve an issue and find a solution.

Child Molestation

Any type of sexual interaction occurring between a child and another person via manipulation, pressure, or physical force for the pleasure of the offender is defined as child sexual abuse. Such measures may include but are not limited to: watching a child undress to become sexually aroused or fondling oneself, masturbating in front of a child, or exposing oneself to a child, whether in person or via nude pictures, taking pornographic pictures of a child, touching, caressing, or rubbing against a child's body for sexual gratification, asking a child to touch, feel or rub another's body (even a doll), and/or his or her own body for the purpose of sexual gratification. Additionally, any completed oral, vaginal, or anal contact, or insertion of any part of an object into a child's vagina or rectum, unless there is a legitimate medical reason to do so.

Sexual Abuse is Illegal

Child abuse is a national crime; it is illegal in all states. Girls and boys of all ages can become victims of child abuse by adults and other children. Many people may view sexual abuse as a crime committed by strangers; however, most children are often violated by someone they know, love, and trust. For example, a parent, grandparent, uncle, aunt, brother or sister, step parent, or other family members not related by blood, just to name a few. This type of abuse does not discriminate, no matter how rich or poor, regardless of a specific religious belief or race, interfamilial sexual abuse can lurk in any setting. Many children have been molested by their neighbors and babysitters. According to some researchers of child sexual abuse, the majority of recorded child abusers are male, but women and girls can and do sexually abuse children, although this type of abuse is rarely reported.

Physical Force is not the Norm for a Sexual Abuser

An abuser often results to tactics such as verbal threats or manipulation. This is mainly because he or she is often an adult whom the child admires or respects and has had a close relationship.

The abuse often happens over a long period of time and is completed slyly. It slowly migrates from less threatening, to more explicit sexual behavior. For instance, a simple kiss on the cheek may turn into a kiss on the lips followed by a caress or fondle. Once the child's trust and or cooperation are gained, the abuser may bribe the child with gifts or special attention to secure the victim's silence. Once the child suspects an act of violation, betrayal, or discomfort, the abuser may threaten to kill the child, himself, family members or the family pet if the abuse is revealed. Other stratagems may be used. For example, the abuser may exclaim "I'll go to jail if you tell" or insinuate the family will break up. That attacker may even tell his or her victim that other siblings or loved ones will be abused if the child does not comply, or that the other child "likes" or "enjoys" being touched. He or she may also make threats to take away a child's "special attention" or privileges if the child tells.

Most children do not tell when they are being abused simply because they are afraid. While under the manipulation of the abuser, he or she can make the child feel like it is their fault. Additionally, many children who are abused are too young to understand they have rights and should report being sexually abused; they may even have a difficult time describing the criminal because of the nature of the crime. Imagine a little girl reporting that her uncle kissed or hugged her. The parent may think that, that small amount of affection is normal. If the parent deems it as normal, then the child may continue to welcome the abuser out of confusion or for fear of losing the relationship of affection, especially from a loved one. Because of these situations, a child may feel guilty or ashamed. A child must understand what normal acts of affection are, along with a great deal of courage to report abuse.

If You Believe Your Child has been Violated

Because of a lack of understanding, a child may speak about or tell of being abused in a direct manner, while others may ask questions or hint around about the situation. Many times the accusations are vague. Other children may tell a friend, neighbor, teacher, or relative. It is not abnormal to determine if sexual abuse has been committed from reading a letter or seeing a drawing by the child. Some parents may suspect something is different based on unusual actions of the child, but a parent may not suspect any abuse until a knock on the door from an investigator is acknowledged.

No matter how a parent has been notified or made aware of the act, researchers have determined that child abuse is not easy to identify. Children have been sexually abused in a variety of ways and react differently to being violated. The behavioral indicators of sexual abuse listed below are only signs of sexual abuse and does not mean that a child is not being abused. These indicators should be the only actions to determine such a delicate, crucial situation. On the other hand, a child may be reacting to a family crisis such as a loss of a close family member, divorce, or any other event a child may feel pain or anguish from. It should also be noted that some children may not have any of these indications.

Possible Signs of Sexual Abuse

- Uncontrollable urge to use the bathroom (wetting the bed, or themselves)
- Nightmares or wanting to stay awake
- Crying in his/her sleep
- Sexual behaviors or acts of being overly affectionate

- Sudden fear of a particular person
- Childish behaviors or acts of regression
- Depression
- Anger or hostility
- Inappropriate behavior at school
- Problems with their friends
- Hurting themselves or others
- Lack of eating or changes in eating habits
- Onset of sudden sickness although a sickness is not prevalent
- Staying away from home or running away
- Law-breaking
- Talk of or attempted suicide

<u>Physical Signs of Sexual Abuse</u>

Perhaps child abuse is not evident. If physical indicators are present, medical attention should be sought out immediately. A physician who is experienced in the investigation of child sexual abuse will be able to assist with this matter. Likely physical signs of sexual abuse may include:
- Ripped or stained clothing
- Difficulty sitting or walking
- Different appearance of the genital area (swelling, rashes, discharge)
- A child paying special attention to the area
- A reoccurring pain in the genital or anal area
- STD (sexually transmitted disease)

Dorothy Hall

My Child has been Molested. What Do I Do?

Many emotions such as shock, horror, or even rage may erupt once you find out that your child has been molested. Denial or doubt is experienced many times over, and then self-blame. Confusion, grief, and betrayal also surface, especially if the abuser is a loved one or close relative. As a result of these wavering feelings, denial may suddenly spring forth, forcing you to choose sides. You also may have difficulty trying to figure out the difference between loyalty, support, or just simply what to do!

It is important to understand that these feelings are normal, and it will be very important to deal with them later when you are not with your child. The needs of your child are pertinent, and you must stay focused on his or her needs. Confession in total privacy is the primary step to your child's recovery. Be careful how you handle the situation because it will have a major influence on how your child reacts, recovers, and heals from this tragic ordeal. You need to make your child feel as if he or she can trust you completely! Possible remedies to assist with the healing process are:

- Stay calm and be supportive.
- Try as hard as possible not to amplify the situation.
- Take your child in your arms and praise your child for telling you.

Although the abuse may not seem to have happened in your mind, denial is not the way to react to this situation: your child needs to feel that you believe him or her. Remember, most children do not lie about such criminal acts. Listening to your child will reassure you of the truth because he or she will be detailed enough for you understand that a child could not "make up" sexual abuse. Children may naturally lie about the predator committing the act due to common fear of the threats made by the real abuser. Additionally, he may even try to cover up or take back a statement made earlier. Your reactions play an important part to the child revealing detailed information about the abuse as well as the abuser. You must remember to listen to and believe your child.

Proceed with caution as you listen to what happened. Your understanding and belief allows the child to believe that he/she can confide in you, and they can trust you to handle the situation. If it turns out that your child is not telling the truth, counseling is an alternative to determining the reason for such a life-altering accusation. Maybe the lie is a result of other family issues. However, you must never think or feel that you can hide or forget about it. If you do not face the abuse or alleged abuser head on, then your failure to tackle it could lead to other problems for you, the child, and other members of the family.

Make your child understand that the abuse was not their fault; it is always the abusers fault. Give them your parental reassurance by telling them that you love them and will try your best to protect them, always. Your child may feel tainted or damaged and that his or her body may never be the same. Let your child know how beautiful and precious they are no matter what has happened to them.

Your Child Will Need Medical Attention

It is imperative that your child receives medical attention if you suspect that he/she has been violated. This medical exam can also assist with providing evidence that will be necessary for prosecution. If you are able to determine that your child has recently been sexually abused, especially within the past 2 to 3 days, the doctors will be able to collect physical evidence via specimen samples, blood work, cultures, etc. Once this proof is collected, Child Protective Services (CPS) and your local law enforcement agency will provide the necessary steps to file a case on your child's behalf. You must also remember that a negative finding does not mean that your child was not abused.

Regardless of being able to detect if your child has been harmed, it is important to have him or her medically examined. Children may believe a part of their body has been damaged or "broken." Thus, obtaining medical reassurance will provide some sort or relief for you and your child.

You should visit a doctor that is trained and experienced with child sexual abuse cases. Your regular pediatrician may not be able to perform the examination, but will be able to refer you to one who can.

Report the Abuse

Depending on which state you live in and the circumstances of the abuse, child sexual abuse may be reported to the local CPS agency or to the police. Both agencies may investigate the report together.

If the abuse was carried out by a stranger or a non-family member, such as a teacher, coach, or babysitter, call the police immediately. However, if the sexual abuse was committed by another person in the household, such as a relative, or a boyfriend or girlfriend of the parent, the incident should be reported to CPS. You can always call the police if the agency is closed.

A county or statewide child abuse hotline should also be available on which to make a report. Check the government section of your local white pages for the telephone number. If you cannot locate the agency, or you need help making the call, a crisis counselor with Childhelp National Child Abuse Hotline may be able to help you. The telephone number is 1-800-4-A-CHILD (1-800-422-4453).

It is likely that the person who abused your child will abuse or has abused other children. Moreover, you have a legal duty to protect your child from harm. Parents have been held liable for failure to protect their children when they chose to place the concerns of others above a child's safety. Placement of your child outside the home, termination of your parental rights, and criminal charges are possible results of failing to protect a child from continued harm. Confronting the abuser without doing anything about it will not stop the abuse, and may place you and your child in greater danger. Therefore, it is in your best interest and the best interest of your child to report the abuse and to discuss the situation with a professional at CPS. Remember, abuse will not stop without intervention.

If you are also being abused, contact a woman's shelter for information and support. A woman's shelter or another advocacy group may be able to provide temporary refuge for you and your children, if you need it.

The Outcome of Reporting Child Sexual Abuse

Based on demographics, child sexual abuse outcomes will vary; it is impossible to tell you the exact outcome, but perhaps the following information will provide you with some insight of what could possibly happen:

An interview may follow after the abuse is reported. A law enforcement officer, an investigator from CPS or both may interview your child. You may be asked a series of questions about your child, family, the actual abuse, and the suspected violator. Based on the information you provide, the reporter will decide whether to proceed with the case. The time span will vary, however, if the agency believes your child is in danger at the present time, the case could start immediately. Most of the time, your child will be interviewed during the beginning of the investigation. The setting or environment of the interview will vary. Once the abused child is investigated, you and other children or family members may be interviewed as well; witnesses may even be subpoenaed.

Videotaping can eliminate the numerous amounts of interviews that often happen with the investigation. Likewise, videotaping can enable a prosecutor to make a decision on whether or not to pursue a case. Of course, videotaping may frighten a child, but with newfound methods of technology, this procedure can be done quickly and discreetly. The time frame of the investigation can range from several weeks to several months. The decision of whether to try the case depends on many reasons. If the prosecutor decides to try the case, an arrest warrant will be issued for the person who allegedly committed the crime. You should also be aware that this person may post bond to get out of jail; he or she may also remain free until the actual court date. The defendant may enter a plea of guilty in an effort to receive a lesser sentence of the crime. However, he or she may also plead not guilty. In this situation, a trial date will be set. Sometimes the trial can be very lengthy and frustrating. Be sure to seek outside counseling or therapy if you feel the need or become overwhelmed.

Please remember: If you are involved with another matter such as abuse or neglect, the judge can appoint someone to be an advocate for your child. Some state laws allow a guardian ad litem to represent the child during the court process. In some states, children are old enough to have their own attorneys represent them. For more information about the services of volunteer guardian ad litem (GAL), contact the court-appointed special advocates association (CASA). The helpline for CASA is 1-800-628-3233 or 206-270-0072.

Can You Recognize the Sign(s) of Abuse?

You can love and want the very best for your children and still unintentionally harm your child. Parents need help sometimes, for parents are void of perfection. Being honest enough to admit and recognize there is a problem takes courage. Recognizing a negative pattern and addressing it can be the start of a new beginning, not only in your child's life, but in yours. Change has the potential to be difficult and frightening. Perhaps it can evoke memories of past abuse and neglect in your own childhood. It is never too late to improve your relationship with your child/ren. Your ability to risk an honest appraisal of your relationship with your child(ren) is a sign of strength.

Are You at Risk of being the Abuser?

The following section provides you with possible ways to determine issues or potential problems with your child. Perhaps you can take the time to improve your relationship. Some of the questions may be far-fetched and offensive. However, this is a critical issue, and remember, realistic information is crucial when dealing with child abuse or neglect. If you feel like you need to change, do not judge yourself; recognizing change is a positive step.

Your natural ability to love, your tenacity and strength is what deems you a parent. Recognizing that there is room for change is major. What may seem surprising is: there are many places to receive support. You are not alone; parenting can be challenging, frustrating, and demanding.

A few questions to assess the challenges that may come along with parenting are:

- Does parenting overwhelm you?
- Do you sometimes feel you need additional support?
- Do you feel depressed or anxious often?
- Do you drink or take any type of drug/painkiller more than you should?
- Have you ever made such remarks to or about your child such as "I wish you were never born!" or "You can't seem to do anything right!"?
- Has the thought ever occurred to you that you might hurt your child?
- Have you ever physically hurt your child?
- Have you ever been question or lied to someone about how your child was injured?
- Have you ever touched your child or any child inappropriately whether bathing or during comforting?
- Have you ever sexually fantasized about a child?

Please refer to chapter twenty-one for helpful information on who to call when you need help for those in crisis that have been sexually abused.

Chapter 21

Organizations Offering Assistance

Help for children, teens, and parents in crisis:
Childhelp National Child Abuse Hotline
1-800-4-A-CHILD
1-800-2-A-CHILD (TDD)

This national hotline is available twenty-four hours a day, seven days a week, to provide crisis counseling. Referrals to child abuse prevention and treatment services, emergency shelter programs. Parenting education, support groups, and other services to victims of child abuse. Parents and others interested in the prevention of child maltreatment.

Boys Town National Hotline
1-800-448-3000
1-800-448-1833 (TDD)

This twenty-four hour national hotline accepts calls from children, teens, and adults about any problem. Including sexual abuse, physical abuse, substance abuse, and gang activity, domestic violence, running away, and parenting problems. Operators can provide counseling and referrals to helpful organizations in your area.

Parents Anonymous National Office
(909) 621-6184

Parents Anonymous is a national self-help organization for parents who are having difficulty parenting. Groups are led by parents and facilitated by professionals in a nonjudgmental environment. Services are free. Call to find out if there is a chapter in your area. You do not have to give your name.

Voices in Action
1-800-7-VOICE-8
(312) 327-1500

Operates twenty-four hours. It is an international organization that provides assistance to victims of incest and child sexual abuse. Provides members with referrals to self-help groups, therapists, and puts you in touch with others who have experienced similar types of abuse. Voices in Action publishes an informational 'survival kit,' a newsletter, and offers national and regional conferences.

National Committee to Prevent Child Abuse
312-663-3520
www.childabuse.org

Dedicated to preventing child abuse in all its forms. NCPA publishes materials, conducts research, and maintains a fifty-state network of chapters.

Dorothy Hall

Author's Suggestions:

1) Check for sex offenders in your town via the Internet or your local courthouse.

2) Don't allow your children to take gifts from strangers.

3) Buy dolls for small children. Sometimes they don't want to talk about it, but they'll express themselves through play.

4) Never let them see that you are afraid of your spouse or anyone else. The predators will use this to their advantage.

5) Look for signs and changes in your child's behavior.

6) Build a solid foundation with your child, letting them know it's okay to come to you with anything.

7) Never judge a book by its cover. Search to find out its contents.

8) Ethnic background doesn't matter. People that sexually abuse children don't discriminate.

9) Never put your child's name on the outside of anything belonging to them. If you do this, it'll allow a stranger to call them on a first name basis, as if they know them or their parents.

For instance, Tim is riding his bike down the street and his book bag is on his back with his name printed as clear as day. The predator sees it today, but doesn't approach him. Tomorrow, Tim leaves the bag home, but he's on the same bike route as yesterday. The predator waits to catch Tim off guard, knowing kids hardly ever think as quickly as adults. The predator calls out his name, and Tim stops to talk, and in a matter of seconds, the predator starts to build a relationship with Tim that's eventually bound for the destruction of Tim's life.

In Conclusion

After reading the stories shared in this book, you now have some knowledge of what goes on behind the doors that you can't see through. It displays the misery, humiliation, and the terror that enters the lives of the innocent by masked molesters.

We need to take heed of what's occurring in our nation today by not letting the wicked steal the joy and the life of our future to be. I have tried my best to get through to you to the best of my ability, enabling you to become aware of heinous acts carried out by masked molesters.

It may not be you, but what about a family member, a neighbor, or just a child crying out for help to adults who neglect to acknowledge what's really going on under their noses? It is our responsibility as adults to protect the children of our future to the best of our ability.

To the masked molesters of our world today, you know who you are. By carrying out these heinous acts, you can't begin to imagine the pain you have or are causing to these children.

Why? How could you?

I beg you, please, no more. How can you ever forgive yourself? Of course, our Father in heaven will forgive you. But you still have to pay accordingly for your actions. Is it worth it? If this thought ever crosses your mind, think twice first. No child deserves this kind of abuse.

References

Hartman, Lauren. 1998. *Solutions: The Woman's Crisis Handbook.* New York: Mariner Books

Retrieved from
http://www.childhelp.org

Retrieved from
http://www.thekidsafefoundation.org

About the Author

Dorothy Hall also writes fiction under the pseudonym Sereniti Hall and was listed in the *Library Journal's* top ten best books for Street Literature 2011. She is currently working on her next project and lives in Augusta, Georgia with her three daughters and husband. You may contact Dorothy Hall at:

E-mail: dorothyhall58@yahoo.com
Facebook: Dorothy Hall
Twitter: dorothyhall58

Reading Group Questions

1. Are you a person who thinks this could never happen in your home?

2. If you answered yes to number one, have you ever judged others that this has happened to?

3. Do you think that people could ever be too careful when it comes to the well-being of their children?

4. Have you talked to your children about molesters or about people that could potentially ask them to keep secrets?

5. What did you get out of this book? Do you feel the book served its purpose?

6. Will you have a talk with your children after reading this book?

7. Do you feel that once a molester has victimized a person, their life can turn for the worse? Drugs, alcoholism, promiscuity, failed relationships, homosexual relationships, violence etc.

8. Will you be one of the people to turn a blind eye and deaf ear, or will you be strong enough to stand up for yourself and your children?

9. Are you a victim and afraid to speak about it?

10. Will you recommend this book to others?